Modern Macroeconomic Analys

C000216664

Modern Macroeconomic Analysis

Paul Turner

Lecturer in Economics
School of Business and Economic
Studies
University of Leeds

McGRAW-HILL BOOK COMPANY

London · New York · St Louis · San Francisco · Auckland
Bogotá · Caracas · Hamburg · Lisbon · Madrid · Mexico · Milan
Montreal · New Delhi · Panama · Paris · San Juan · São Paulo
Singapore · Sydney · Tokyo · Toronto

Published by
McGRAW-HILL Book Company Europe
Shoppenhangers Road, Maidenhead, Berkshire, SL6 2QL, England
Telephone 0628 23432
Fax 0628 770224

British Library Cataloguing in Publication Data

Turner, Paul
    Modern Macroeconomic Analysis
    I. Title
    339

    ISBN 0–07–707717–2

Library of Congress Cataloging-in-Publication Data

Turner, Paul.
    Modern macroeconomic analysis / Paul Turner.
        p.   cm.
    Includes bibliographical references and index.
    ISBN 0–07–707717–2
    1. Macroeconomics.   I. Title.
HB172.5.T784   1993
339–dc20

Copyright © 1993 McGraw-Hill International (UK) Limited. All rights reserved. No
part of this publication may be reproduced, stored in a retrieval system, or
transmitted, in any form or by any means, electronic, mechanical, photocopying,
recording, or otherwise, without the prior permission of McGraw-Hill International
(UK) Limited.

1234 CUP 9543

Typeset by Datix International Limited, Bungay, Suffolk
Printed in Great Britain at the University Press, Cambridge

Contents

Preface

This book derives from the lecture courses in macroeconomics that I have given at the universities of Leeds and Southampton. It is designed to be used by undergraduate students who have completed a typical first-year course in that it is assumed that they have completed preliminary courses in economics, mathematics and statistics. While the book is suitable primarily for second-year undergraduate courses, some of the later chapters may be of interest to final-year students.

My main reason for writing this book has been the conviction that the most important skill a macroeconomist needs to acquire is the ability to think in terms of, and manipulate, small formal models of the economy. Therefore, the book begins with models and techniques which are relatively familiar, such as the comparative static analysis of Keynesian and Classical economic theory, and proceeds to less familiar areas such as the dynamic analysis of inflation. In terms of theory, I have tried to be non-committal in the hope that students can use the analysis presented to make up their own minds about which is the most appropriate way to model the economy; but the balance of material probably reflects my own interest in the New Keynesian macroeconomics.

Another major factor influencing the way in which this book has been written has been a growing belief that it is impossible to separate macroeconomic theory and empirical work at any level of the subject. If we are ever to put macroeconomics on any sort of scientific footing then we must confront our theories with data, and if this is the case, then we should be training our students to get into the habit of doing this as early as possible. Most of the material in this book therefore combines theory and evidence in an attempt to get students to appreciate the process by which the two are synthesized.

This book divides into two main sections. The first comprises Chapters 1 to 4 and adopts a systems approach. The objective of this section is to put forward working models of the economy which embody the alternative theoretical perspectives in existence. Chapter 1 begins by describing the phenomena which theory seeks to explain. The recent literature on the separation of trend and cyclical components in macroeconomic time series is reviewed and its implications for the types of theory we might wish to consider are discussed. This chapter contains perhaps the most technically demanding material in the book. Although it provides an introduction to some of the most up-to-date research in the subject it may prove tough going for those students without a strong mathematical background. For that reason, it can be safely omitted without loss of continuity when reading the book. The reader can then treat the rest of the book as an entity in its own right or return to Chapter 1 after the rest of the material has been mastered.

In Chapter 2 we set out some theories of economic growth which are relevant to explaining the permanent, or trend, behaviour of the macroeconomic aggregates of interest. We then move on in Chapters 3 and 4 to consider short-run macroeconomic models of the transitory, or cyclical, components of macroeconomic variables. Here the emphasis is on models in which the period of time considered is sufficiently short to treat the capital stock as fixed. Chapter 3 concentrates on Classical approaches to the business cycle, emphasizing those based on imperfect price information, i.e. the Lucas 'price-surprise' approach, and those based on technology shocks, the 'real business cycle' approach. Chapter 4 considers the short-run Keynesian model, emphasizing the role of government policy as a correction for market failure.

The second section, which comprises Chapters 5 to 8, contains discussions of the microfoundations of the macroeconomic relationships which go to make up the systems models. It is here where much of the recent research in New Keynesian economics has made its distinctive contribution. By modifying the constraints facing agents and allowing for the existence of imperfect competition a role for Keynesian macroeconomic policy of the traditional kind has been reintroduced. Chapter 5 analyses the wage- and price-setting process. It is arguable that it is here where the major difference between the New Keynesian and New Classical approaches arises. New Classical economists have, on the whole, been content to work within a framework of flexible prices and perfect competition in both goods and labour markets. New Keynesian models reject both these assumptions and thus attempt to provide microfoundations for the kinds of nominal stickiness which underlie the Keynesian macroeconomic model discussed in Chapter 4. We concentrate on three main issues: 'near-rational' equilibrium models, the efficiency wage model and the overlapping contracts version of the traditional Phillips curve. Chapter 6 discusses the consumption and investment functions. The emphasis here is on deriving both these relationships using the principles of utility maximization as a basis. The effects of market imperfections, such as liquidity constraints, are also discussed in some detail. Chapter 7 analyses the monetary sector of the economy, again emphasizing the determination of the demand for money in terms of utility maximization. Finally, Chapter 8 discusses the open economy, with particular emphasis on the issue of exchange-rate overshooting in foreign exchange markets.

To provide links between economic theory and practical problems, each chapter contains two separate units which describe issues of interest or applications of the main body of material. These may be used as examples by lecturers to deepen students' understanding. While some of these units cover very recent research, others concentrate on 'classic' applications or pieces of empirical research.

The choice of topics considered is necessarily selective. Research in macroeconomics has been extraordinarily active over the last two decades, in no small part due to the stimulus provided by the New Classical challenge to the Keynesian orthodoxy. I hope that students using this book will find my choice of topic interesting and informative but they should remember that there are vast areas of the subject left relatively untouched by this text. I would be very pleased if this book went some way towards providing them with the background to read further into the subject and the interest to do so.

Introduction

The nature of macroeconomics

The aim of this introduction is to give a perspective on the subject matter of the book before the overall view becomes obscured by detailed discussion. The first necessary step is to provide a definition of what macroeconomics constitutes. My view is that macroeconomics consists of the study of the joint behaviour of any set of economic aggregates of interest. Note the emphasis on the *joint* rather than simply individual behaviour of aggregates. Macroeconomics is essentially a branch of general equilibrium theory in that it seeks to explain the simultaneous behaviour of variables which are linked through accounting, technological and behavioural relationships. In any developed macroeconomic model all three types of relationship play an important role, but the key step is undoubtedly the specification of the behavioural relationships which are designed to model the choices and actions of broad groups of agents within the economy. Accounting and technological relationships are necessary and important, but it is the analysis of behaviour which distinguishes economics from other disciplines.

Readers may well wonder why I have not specified the reasons for our interest in the joint behaviour of economic variables in my definition. This is not an omission but a recognition that economists differ in this matter. For many years it would have been automatically understood that the source of interest in macroeconomic models was ultimately the design of government economic policy, for the purposes of stabilizing the economy and promoting growth. Thus the desire to *control* the path of the economy was taken for granted. Over the last two decades this view has come under attack, and the belief in the ability of government to achieve a reasonable level of control over the economy, once taken for granted, has diminished. The New Classical version of macroeconomics gives control very low priority. Macroeconomic models are still necessary for the purposes of understanding the economy and forecasting its likely future path, in much the same way as meteorological models are necessary for weather forecasting. However, attempts to control the economy are argued to be as futile as attempts to control the weather.

Alternative paradigms

The New Classical research programme came as a welcome antidote to the overconfidence of many macroeconomists in their ability to manipulate the economy. It is arguable, however, that the case for the impotence of government has been overstated. Economic systems are not weather systems, they arise out of economic decisions taken by individual agents and, as such, these decisions can be affected by the state in numerous different ways. This does not mean that designing policy is likely to be easy. Indeed, many New Classical theorists would argue that it is the fact that agents are intelligent, optimizing individuals, who alter their behaviour in reaction to government policy, that makes policy design so difficult and unpredictable. However, even in the most liberal of economies, government tends to be the largest single economic agent, and therefore its actions must necessarily have important repercussions for the behaviour of other individuals and groups of agents.

Given my arguments so far, I have adopted the strategy that the first role of this book should be to provide models which are capable of describing the economy, and to tackle issues of economic control and policy only when a suitable descriptive model has been set out. Thus Keynesian issues of fiscal and monetary policies are only dealt with once it has been established, through the use of a descriptive model, that market failures are sufficiently important to make them feasible and desirable. In placing the emphasis on description we need to make some judgement as to what features of the behaviour of economic variables we wish to describe. This is the subject matter of Chapter 1 but, to pre-empt this discussion, we can say here that the main features of the time-series behaviour of economic aggregates, which theory must seek to explain, are the existence of long-run trends and short-run fluctuations around these trends. Macroeconomic theory has traditionally concentrated on the latter, but a recent revival in growth theory has seen emphasis shift to the explanation of trend rather than cycle.

The above paragraphs have hinted at the alternative paradigms employed by macroeconomists and which act as the major source of disagreement and argument among them. These are not simply competing models of the economy but competing philosophies of the design of macroeconomic models. New Classical macroeconomics takes as its basis the hypothesis that all agents are rational utility-maximizing agents *and* that the price mechanism coordinates the actions of these agents so as to achieve a Pareto-efficient outcome for the economy as a whole. For the most part, Keynesian macroeconomists would accept the first part of the above statement but reject the second, arguing that there are inherent rigidities in the operation of markets which prevent adjustment to a full Pareto-efficient outcome in the short, and even the long, run. This difference between the two schools of thought appears to be irreconcilable and untestable. It is difficult to think of any experiment or other empirical test which would convince either camp of the falsity of its position. For the benefit of the reader, the author's sympathies lie with the Keynesian position but the rigour and discipline which the New Classical revolution has forced onto the economic profession as a whole is worthy of great respect.

It may seem excessively gloomy to emphasize the theoretical divide which separates macroeconomists into two groups. However, this would be misleading. In many ways, the existence of two rival schools of thought has been to the benefit of both. The problems and objections raised by one school to the hypotheses put forward by the other have prevented either becoming complacent and have stimulated a healthy development of both. This is nowhere more evident than in the development of New Keynesian macroeconomics, which seeks to explain Keynesian phenomena, such as the existence of involuntary unemployment and the adjustment of real quantities in response to nominal shocks, by using the hypothesis of rational utility-maximizing individuals as a basis. Thus the New Keynesian school has adopted much of the technology brought into the profession by the New Classicists but has taken seriously market imperfections which give rise to inefficient macroeconomic outcomes.

Besides considering issues of high theory, this book also has a more mundane aim. To be a functioning macroeconomist it is necessary to acquire a 'tool-kit' of models and techniques which can be applied to a variety of different economic situations. Again, this is an area where different theoretical perspectives seem to play little role. Both Keynesian and New Classical economists make use of many of the same concepts. It is possible to demonstrate examples of the use of the Phillips curve, the *IS* curve and the assumption of rational expectations in papers by members of either group. A major part of this book is therefore to equip the student with the tools used in common by macroeconomists of all types. At the risk of mixing metaphors, an alternative analogy would be that all economists use the same basic language to express very different ideas. However, it is necessary to learn how to speak the language before one can enter the debate.

Acknowledgements

Thanks are due to a number of colleagues without whom this book would never have been completed. First, I would like to thank my commissioning editor, Brendan Lambon, who has reminded me at intervals that submission deadlines were due and gently pushed me into getting on with the job. On the academic side I would like to thank Sue Bowden, Andrew Coutts, Jenny Roberts and Terry Mills for the opportunity to discuss serious academic economics with them during regular lunchtime research workshops. Finally, I would like to thank my wife, Gaby, and my two daughters, Rachel and Catherine, who may find that my temper improves now that the book is finished.

Paul Turner

1.
Trends and cycles in macroeconomic data

In this chapter we will consider the nature of macroeconomic time series. We have already seen that macroeconomics consists of the study of economic aggregates such as the levels of output and unemployment. An important part of this is the explanation of the past behaviour of these aggregates. Indeed, a great deal of the raw material of macroeconomics comes in the form of *time-series data*. A time series consists of a set of observations on a variable which are indexed by time. As we shall see, the properties of such data are quite different from those of the random sample which is usually assumed in elementary statistical analysis.

The first section of this chapter considers the behaviour of some important economic variables over the last century and a half. We look at how output, employment and the capital stock have evolved through time, and argue that these series exhibit a number of features common to many macroeconomic time series. The second part sets out a more formal framework for the analysis of time series. The key issue here is whether the behaviour of the variable in question can be split into trend and cyclical components. This issue has stimulated much debate in recent years and is still the subject of some controversy. We then consider explicitly the alternative models which have been suggested to implement the trend–cycle split and show how they can be applied to the time series described in Sec. 1.1. The economic significance of this debate is then considered and we ask whether it contributes to the resolution of any important theoretical controversies. Finally, we bring the argument up to date by examining some recent controversies over the relative importance of trends and cycles in the data.

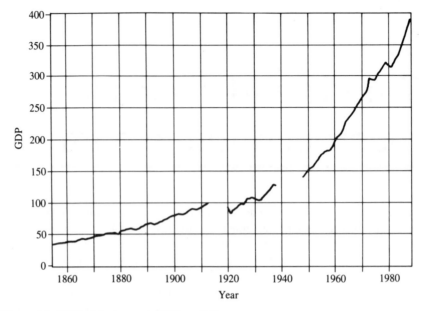

Figure 1.1 GDP at factor cost (1913 = 100)

1.1 Characteristics of macroeconomic time series

Thanks to the important work of a number of economic historians and statisticians, macroeconomists now have access to long runs of historical data on many interesting economic variables. In this section we look at three: the levels of output, employment and the capital stock. Taken together, these form the basis of a simple but interesting model of economic growth which can tell us much about the performance of the UK economy.

Let us begin by considering the level of output. Figure 1.1 shows an index of Gross Domestic Product (GDP) at factor cost over the period 1855 to 1988. The periods corresponding to the two world wars have been omitted because they distort severely the behaviour of the series. During wartime the economy was run at a very high level of capacity utilization, labour was directed towards particular occupations and women, who were not normally part of the labour force, were drawn into employment. The net effect of this was to produce temporary boosts in output which could not be sustained in a peacetime environment. Thus inclusion of the war years would make the series appear far more erratic than it really is.

The most obvious properties of the data shown in Fig. 1.1 are the existence of a strong trend in output throughout the period coupled with fluctuations around the trend path. The apparent acceleration of growth shown in the shape of the curve is the result of graphing the data in level

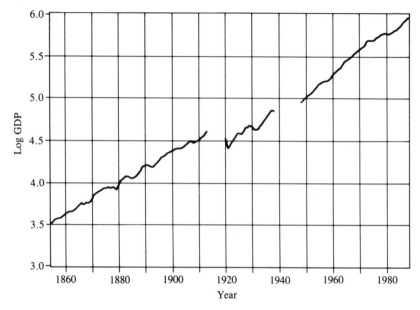

Figure 1.2 GDP at factor cost (log scale)

terms. With a constant proportional growth rate (or exponential growth), the level of any series will exhibit the upward curve shown in Fig. 1.1. To obtain a more accurate picture of whether the growth rate accelerates, economists often make use of diagrams drawn on a *semi-log* scale. Such a diagram is given in Fig. 1.2, which relates the natural logarithm of our GDP series to time. We can see clearly from this graph that the growth rate has not accelerated significantly through time in the way that a careless interpretation of Fig. 1.1 might lead us to believe.

There is an obvious discontinuity in the data after the First World War in that, if we extrapolated the pre-1913 trend, we would obtain a huge overestimate of post-war GDP. This can be partly explained by the removal of the 26 counties of (the Republic of) Ireland from the UK data after 1920 following partition but, even taking this into account, there remains a substantial unexplained shortfall. Of course, familiarity with the economic history of the period should make us aware that the early-1920s were years of severe depression for the UK. The behaviour of GDP after the Second World War contrasts with this. No major depression occurred in the late 1940s (much to the suprise of many contemporary observers).

Why has GDP grown in the manner shown by Figs 1.1 and 1.2? Economic theory, at its most simple, attempts to answer this question by means of an *aggregate production function*. This relates output (GDP) to inputs of

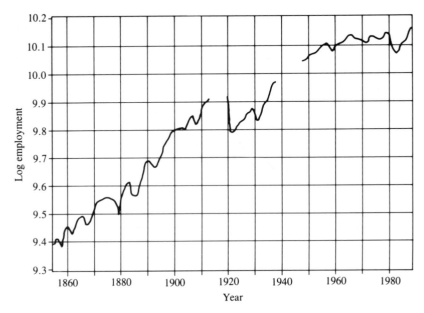

Figure 1.3 Employees in employment (log scale)

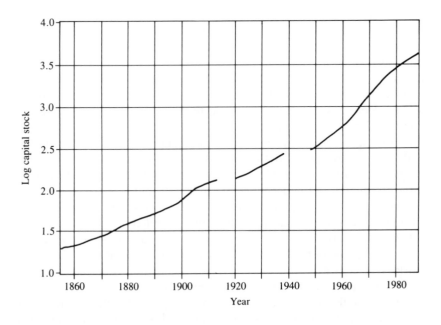

Figure 1.4 Capital stock (log scale)

factors of production (employment and capital). Graphs of employment and capital for the UK economy over the same period as the graphs for GDP are given in Figs 1.3 and 1.4. It is evident that there has been strong growth in both series, though the growth rate of employment slows down significantly after the Second World War. Is the growth in factor inputs sufficient in itself to explain the growth of output? To answer this question we need to move beyond simple examination of the data and make use of some economic theory by assuming a specific kind of production function.

The simplest aggregate production function to work with is the *constant-returns Cobb–Douglas production function*. This can be written algebraically as:

$$Y_t = A_t K_t^\alpha N_t^{1-\alpha} \tag{1.1}$$

where Y, K and N are output, capital and labour, respectively, and A is a scale parameter which can be given an interpretation in terms of the productivity of factor inputs. The exponent α reflects the contribution of capital relative to labour in the production process, and is usually estimated by taking the share of capital in total factor receipts. If we take logarithms of Eq. (1.1) and express it in first difference then we get an equation in growth rates:

$$\Delta \ln Y_t = \Delta \ln A_t + \alpha \Delta \ln K_t + (1 - \alpha)\Delta \ln N_t \tag{1.2}$$

This equation provides a basis for decomposing the growth rate of output into that part which can be explained by increases in factors of production and that which is due to unexplained changes in their productivity. The usual procedure is to construct a measure of the growth rate of Total Factor Input (TFI) by taking a weighted average of the growth rates of labour and capital (here we set the weight on capital equal to 0.3). Once this has been done, we can subtract the growth rate of TFI from that of GDP to get a measure of productivity growth. This is usually referred to as the Solow Residual, following the important paper by Robert Solow (1957), which introduced this technique. It should be noted that Eq. (1.2) is effectively an identity when we use it to define the Solow Residual in this manner. Thus while it may provide a useful starting point in an analysis of productivity growth it cannot, by itself, supply an explanation. Bearing this in mind, we can apply this method to the data in Figs 1.1 to 1.4 to see if the pattern of UK growth has changed significantly through time. The results are shown in Table 1.1.

The acceleration in growth during the 1949–73 period is clearly evident from Table 1.1. The main contributing factors to this appear to have been a very rapid growth rate of capital relative to earlier periods and an increase in the Solow Residual. This is part of a long-term trend in which the contribution of the growth in the labour force to overall growth has fallen

Table 1.1 Growth patterns in the UK economy (compound growth rates: per cent per annum)

Period	Y	N	K	TFI	Solow Residual
1856–1913	1.86	0.89	1.444	1.05	0.81
1921–38	2.59	1.06	1.63	1.25	1.36
1949–73	3.01	0.34	3.18	1.19	1.82
1974–88	1.84	0.24	2.52	0.90	0.93
1949–88	2.56	0.29	2.92	1.08	1.48
Whole period	1.84	0.57	1.77	0.93	0.91

to just a third of its level in the late nineteenth century. Such a pattern is observed in many mature industrial economies where demographic changes have reduced the possibility of generating growth simply by employing more workers.

1.2 Trends and cycles in macroeconomic data

Section 1.1 concentrated on the long-run properties of the series in question, i.e. the behaviour of the trend growth rate. In this section we look at the second major characteristic of the data—the fluctuations of the series around the trend. The separation of economic time series into trend and cycle has long been a focus of interest among economic statisticians. Morgan (1990) discusses the historical evolution of methods used to detrend data for the purposes of both business cycle and demand analysis, while Mills (1990) provides a more technical discussion of the statistical methodologies which have been put forward. We will develop our analysis of trends and cycles within the *unobserved components model*.[1] Any observed series can be conceptually separated into a series of unobserved components, as shown by

$$y_t = \text{Trend}_t + \text{Cyclical}_t + \text{Seasonal}_t + \text{Random}_t \qquad (1.3)$$

The trend component consists of the permanent component of the data, i.e. that portion of the observed value of the series which can be expected to persist through time. In contrast, the cyclical component is composed of temporary deviations from the trend which are nevertheless predictable from the past behaviour of the series. For example, the cyclical component could describe the adjustment of GDP back to its trend growth path following a recession. The seasonal component is included to capture the fact that many economic time series have a regular seasonal pattern, e.g. output falls during holiday periods. Finally, the random component consists of innovations or disturbances to the time series in question.

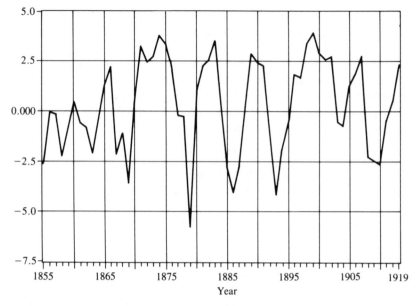

Figure 1.5 Percentage deviations of GDP from trend

In the cases of the time series included here the seasonal component is not important, since the data are reported on an annual basis. This enables us to concentrate on the question of the separation of the data into trend and cycle. Most approaches to this question have attempted to achieve this separation by some form of *detrending* procedure. Examples of this are the use of moving averages, or the regression of the data on a time trend, to estimate the trend component. Once this has been done, the residuals form an estimate of the combined cyclical and random components. These procedures are now recognized as fraught with statistical pitfalls, which will be discussed in the following section. Nevertheless, under certain limiting circumstances, they may provide a valid method of decomposing the data.

One case in which the use of regression on a linear trend can be shown to be valid concerns the behaviour of GDP prior to 1914. Suppose we regress the log of GDP on a constant and time over the period 1855–1913. The equation obtained is of the form:

$$y_t = 3.52 + 0.018t \tag{1.4}$$

where the lower-case y indicates that the dependent variable is a natural logarithm. The residuals from this equation, plotted in Fig. 1.5, are the sum of the cyclical and random components in the log of GDP. As the figure shows, there appears to be a definite cyclical pattern to the residuals, though, as we will argue in the next section, apparent patterns of this kind can be very deceptive.

The decomposition of the time series into its component parts can be taken further by explicitly modelling the cyclical component. A functional form which is capable of generating cyclical patterns is given by a second-order autoregressive process. If such a process is fitted to the residual series an equation of the following form is obtained:

$$yd_t = 0.695yd_{t-1} - 0.253yd_{t-2} \qquad (1.5)$$

where yd are the residuals from Eq. (1.4).

This will generate cycles if the roots of the second-order difference equation defined by Eq. (1.5) are a pair of complex conjugates. This is in fact the case, since the roots can be calculated to be $0.347 \pm 0.364i$.

1.3 Stochastic and deterministic trends in macroeconomic time series

Until the early 1980s the procedure described in Sec. 1.2 was pretty well universal practice among applied economists and was simply assumed to be correct. For example, in his classic paper on business cycle methodology, Lucas (1977) describes the behaviour of output series as follows: 'Technically, movements about trend in gross national product in any country can be well described by a stochastically disturbed difference equation of very low order.' It is not surprising that this methodology achieved such dominance. As we noted in Sec. 1.1, the presence of a strong trend in the data is often the first feature of the data that is evident to an observer. However, in the early 1980s this procedure was challenged in an important paper by Nelson and Plosser (1982).

Nelson and Plosser's (hereafter NP) critique of the prevailing method of detrending data requires us to make use of the concept of *stationarity*. A time series is said to be stationary if it has constant mean and variance.[2] It is obvious that most economic time series are not stationary in this sense since the expected value, or mean, of the series will normally increase through time. However, the process of detrending the data by regression on a linear trend can be seen as a way of allowing for the time-varying mean. Once the effects of growth have been allowed for in this way, the residuals, which, we have argued, include both cyclical and random effects, should consist of a stationary series. Series which can be detrended in this way are described as being *trend stationary*.

It is the assumption that the residuals from a regression on a time trend are stationary that forms the basis of NP's critique of then-prevailing methodology. They propose an alternative to the trend stationary model, namely, the case of *difference stationarity*. Let us suppose that the behaviour of output can be described by an equation of the form:

$$y_t = \gamma + y_{t-1} + \varepsilon_t \tag{1.6}$$

The ε term comprises random disturbances to the series and is usually assumed to be normally distributed with mean zero. Such an equation has a long tradition in the literature on time series and is termed a *random walk with drift*. An alternative terminology is to describe Eq. (1.6) as a *stochastic trend* process while an equation of the form of (1.4) would be described as a *deterministic trend* process. If the first-difference operator is applied to Eq. (1.6) then the result is a stationary process with mean γ and variance σ_ε^2. If we set γ equal to the average growth rate of output, say around 0.02, and simulate the behaviour of Eq. (1.6) in response to random disturbances, then the results generated will look very similar to those from a deterministic trend process subject to random shocks. It is therefore hard to tell whether a series is trend or difference stationary simply by looking at it.

Does it matter whether we assume a series to be trend or difference stationary? The answer to this is, very definitely, yes. Trend stationary processes have the property that deviations from the trend growth path eventually disappear. For example, a boost to aggregate demand may temporarily increase output, but subsequent growth will be lower, and the economy will eventually converge back onto a fixed growth path. This property is referred to as *trend reversion*. In the case of a difference stationary series no such fixed growth path exists. Alternatively, there are an infinite number of growth paths and random disturbances have the effect of moving the economy from one to another. NP argue that in fact most macroeconomic time series of interest are difference rather than trend stationary.[3] Thus the assumption that disturbances have temporary effects on the economy which are eventually reversed is not borne out by the data.

The second major consequence of assuming that a process is trend stationary, when it is difference stationary, is that the residuals will exaggerate the effects of the cycle and may even produce spurious cycles where none exist. This result was developed in a somewhat technical paper by Nelson and Kang (1981). Thus the apparent cycles in economic series which have been a focus of interest for economists for nearly two centuries may simply be the product of an inappropriate statistical technique.

This problem is extremely serious in practice. Although the GDP series for 1855–1913 that we analysed in Sec. 1.2 does appear to be trend stationary, GDP in subsequent periods is better represented by a difference stationary process. This can be confirmed using formal statistical tests for unit roots in the series. Thus the trade cycle, which was such a dominant feature of the late nineteenth-century economy, seems to have disappeared after the First World War. Although the term 'cycle' is still used in the context of stochastic trend models it often means little more than the random component of the series in question.

1.4 The economic implications of stochastic trends

Early papers using the stochastic trend methodology tended to view the presence of such a trend in the data as evidence in favour of the *real business cycle* (RBC) theory. This theory emphasizes the importance of real—usually productivity—shocks over monetary shocks in the generation of economic fluctuations. The argument can be summarized as follows:

1. Macroeconomic theorists are fairly unanimous in agreement with the proposition that money is neutral in the long run, in the sense that an increase in the money stock may have temporary effects on output and employment but that these will subsequently be reversed.
2. Real shocks such as shifts in the aggregate production function due to changes in productivity will have permanent effects on output.
3. The time-series characteristics of output are such that innovations in output are persistent, i.e. a shock to output in one period leads to permanently higher future expected levels of output. This means that the behaviour of output is consistent with the hypothesis that productivity shocks are the main source of innovations rather than monetary shocks.

This is essentially a New Classical approach to explaining business fluctuations (see Chapter 3) since the sources of disturbances are changes in the supply-side potential of the economy rather than shocks to aggregate demand. It differs radically from most other theories of the business cycle in that fluctuations in employment and output are argued to be Pareto-optimal responses to changes in the technology available to producers.[4] If the real business cycle theory is to explain aggregate fluctuations then its proponents must demonstrate the existence of significant fluctuations in productivity. Prescott (1986) has used the Solow Residual for the US economy as a basis for arguing that such fluctuations can be detected. Similar calculations for the UK, as illustrated by Fig. 1.6, also indicate major variations in productivity.

Mankiw (1989) has argued forcibly against the use of the Solow Residual as a measure of cyclical variations in productivity. In his view, the cause of the fluctuations in measured productivity lies in the intensity with which factors of production are used rather than their true productivity. For example, during a recession firms may 'hoard' labour in the expectation of a subsequent upturn. Thus with demand and output falling, but the labour

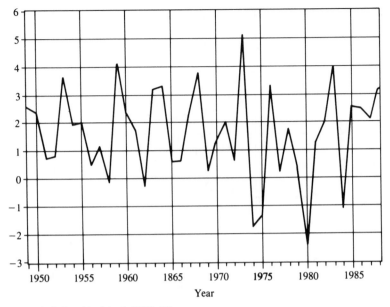

Figure 1.6 Solow Residual, 1949–88

force not adjusting fully, the measured productivity of labour falls. Similarly, during a boom firms may bring into use labour and capital which had been under-utilized previously. Certainly, there is a good correlation between the Solow Residual and the change in output over the previous year, as shown in Fig. 1.7. However, this is also consistent with the hypothesis that underlying productivity growth is responsible for major changes in output growth. This debate has not yet been settled conclusively, empirical evidence being consistent with both hypotheses. Mankiw offers a less formal argument against the RBC interpretation of the productivity data in that we are not given any convincing explanation of the causes of the major shifts in productivity which RBC exponents claim to have identified. While one can certainly point to major events, such as the 1973 and 1979 oil price shocks, which have a detectable influence on productivity, there do not seem to be equally obvious explanations of any of the significant changes occurring in other years.

Explanations for the existence of stochastic trends in macroeconomic time series in a more Keynesian tradition have also been put forward. Before the present debate even started, Tobin (1980) argued that the assertion that demand-side policies have strictly temporary effects on the level of real output is simply false. His argument is that sustained periods of depression result in the deterioration of the skills embodied in the workforce (the stock of *human capital*) and that this damages the long-run supply

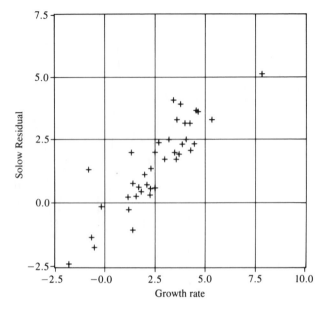

Figure 1.7 Solow Residual and growth rate

potential of the economy. Blanchard and Summers (1986) have made use of the idea of *hysteresis* in the labour market. Their argument is that a disturbance to aggregate demand which increases the level of unemployment will not have a merely temporary effect since it will also cause the *natural rate of unemployment* to rise. This is because, if unemployed for long enough, workers become detached from the labour force and cease to compete effectively for jobs. In models where hysteresis is present the natural rate of unemployment is not an unchanging constant, determined by the fundamentals of the labour market, but a dynamic variable which changes through time as a result of the actual history of unemployment. Unit 5.1 on page 95 provides a more extended discussion of the phenomenon of hysteresis along with an assessment of its importance in the US and European economies.

The general conclusion of this section must therefore be that, even if it is accepted that macroeconomic time series are best described in terms of a stochastic trend, and that disturbances therefore have permanent effects on aggregates of interest, this does not act as convincing proof of the greater relevance of real business cycle theory over the Keynesian alternative. RBC explanations for these properties have figured prominently in the literature but suffer from a number of inherently implausible features. Alternative explanations in the Keynesian tradition are equally capable of explaining the important features of the data.

1.5 Segmented trends, interventions and the cycle

We have seen that if NP's claim that most economic time series are difference stationary is correct then this has profound implications for our view of the business cycle. The central point is that the use of a deterministic trend to model a process, which is in fact difference stationary, will overstate the importance of the cycle and even produce spurious cycles. Under the assumption of difference stationarity, far more of the fluctuations in any given series can be explained by movements in the trend or 'permanent' component of the series.

Arguments against these propositions have been put forward in two recent papers by Perron (1989) and Rappoport and Reichlin (1989). In both papers the idea that *all* disturbances have permanent effects on the expected future level of macroeconomic time series is questioned. While there are a limited number of large identifiable shocks which can be shown to have had such effects, the normal pattern is for disturbances to die out and the economy to return to a trend growth path. Large disturbances can be modelled in two ways. The first is by the use of an *intervention*, a once-and-for-all shift in the level of the function, leaving the slope unchanged. The second method is that of a *segmented trend*, which constitutes a change in the slope of the function, i.e. the growth rate of the variable concerned.

Both Perron and Rappoport and Reichlin re-examine the NP data set using a combination of interventions and breaks in trend. Perron uses a single intervention to account for the 1929 crash and a break in trend to explain the slowdown in growth after the 1973 oil shock. Rappoport and Reichlin use a series of breaks in trend to account for major shocks. In both cases the conclusions are that many of the series identified as difference stationary by NP are better modelled as trend stationary, subject to the more sophisticated specifications of the trend outlined above. The conclusions of Rappoport and Reichlin are worth quoting directly:

> Many quantity series seem to be adequately parameterised by segmented trends, which undergo intermittent shocks, between which they behave as trend stationary processes. ... One interpretation of these results is that the permanent shocks identified by real business cycle models do not occur sufficiently frequently to account for observed business fluctuations. (1989, page 176)

1.6 Conclusions

In this chapter we have examined the ways in which economists model the behaviour of macroeconomic time series. The division between trend and cycle has been an important part of applied macroeconomic research for as long as macroeconomics has existed. The challenge to established method put forward by Nelson and Plosser therefore has implications which are potentially extremely wide reaching. Although the alleged presence of stochastic trends in the data has been used as an argument in favour of real business cycle models, we have argued that more conventional Keynesian interpretations are possible. Thus we would contend that the presence of a stochastic trend in the data does not imply the automatic superiority of either explanation of the business cycle. The importance of this property lies in its implications for empirical modelling rather than the debates between different theoretical schools of thought. Recent research has challenged NP's findings on the grounds that many of the series they identify as being difference stationary can be adequately modelled as being trend stationary with a limited number of interventions and/or breaks in trend.

Unit 1.1

Unit roots and the persistence of shocks

In the main text we have shown that the presence of a unit root in a time series is important when decomposing it into trend and cyclical components. A related topic of importance is the degree to which shocks are persistent when a unit root is present, by which we mean to what extent a shock to the series influences our forecast of the value of the series over any given future time horizon.

If a series is trend stationary then, by definition, shocks have purely temporary effects. Since the variable must eventually converge back onto its deterministic trend growth path it must be the case that disturbances to it have no persistence. Suppose, however, that the series has a unit root. Does this mean that shocks to it are persistent in the sense that they permanently raise our forecasts of its future value by the same amount? Campbell and Mankiw (1987) have shown that this is not necessarily the case. Consider a simple example of a series with a unit root (i.e. one which must be differenced to make it stationary) and a first-order moving average component:

$$\Delta y_t = \varepsilon_t - \theta\varepsilon_{t-1} \qquad\qquad\qquad (U1.1.1)$$

The long-run effect on y of a unit disturbance to ε is given by $(1 - \theta)$. This means that although a unit root is present in the series, disturbances have very little persistence if θ is close to unity.

In practice, most economic time series seem to exhibit a very high degree of persistence. Campbell and Mankiw estimate a whole range of ARIMA models (i.e. models which contain a mixture of autoregressive and moving-average components applied to a series which has been differenced sufficient times to make it stationary) for US Real Gross National Product and find that, if anything, it exhibits excess persistence. This means that a 1 per cent disturbance to GNP raises the long-run future expectation of GNP by more than 1 per cent.

Similarly, for the UK there is no evidence to suggest that fluctuations in GDP are transitory. The following equation gives an estimated first-order moving-average equation for the first difference of annual GDP over the period 1951–88:

$$\Delta y_t = 0.0249 + \varepsilon_t + 0.0843\varepsilon_{t-1} \qquad \text{(U1.1.2)}$$
$$\quad\;\; (0.003) \quad\;\; (0.167)$$

Standard errors are in parentheses.

The moving-average coefficient is very small and insignificantly different from zero, indicating that the series is very close to a random walk with drift. In terms of persistence, this means that a 1 per cent shock to current GDP raises our long-run expected value by 1 per cent. There is certainly no evidence of any tendency for the effects of the disturbance to die out with time.

Unit 1.2

Comovements between series

In describing the business cycle it is necessary to take into account the relationships between the deviations from trend of economic time series, as well as the patterns of these deviations for the individual series. These relationships between series are known as *comovements*. Generally, we categorize each series by comparing its cyclical movement with that of aggregate output. Series which exhibit a positive deviation from trend when the output deviation is positive are said to be *pro-cyclical*, while those which exhibit a negative deviaton are said to be *counter-cyclical*. Similarly, if a series tends to have cyclical peaks which precede those of the output series it is said to *lead* the cycle, whereas if these peaks occur after those in output it is said to *lag* the cycle.

During the 1920s there was considerable interest in using data to establish a set of benchmark facts about business cycles which were not tied to any particular theoretical standpoint. Business cycle facts simply consist of the time-series characteristics of the variables concerned, i.e. the means, variances and covariances, along with the pattern of comovements between the series. This approach can be seen most clearly in the work of Wesley Mitchell for the National Bureau of Economic Research. However, in later years, this was largely abandoned in favour of research programmes which investigated the business cycle through the use of a specific theoretical framework (in particular, the Keynesian multiplier–accelerator model).

In recent years the business cycle facts literature appears to have made something of a comeback. Kydland and Prescott (1990) have conducted a study along these lines for the US economy while Blackburn and Ravn (1990) have replicated, and extended, their work for the UK. This work has made extensive use of a relatively new method of separating out trend and cycle in the data, which has become known as the *Hodrick–Prescott filter*. This assumes that the trend in the series can be captured by a smooth, continuous line through the data, but that the slope of this line can change through time. Thus, application of this filter to UK real GDP data produces a trend line of the kind shown by the broken line in Fig. U1.2.1. The cycle is then taken to be the deviations of actual GDP from this trend line, as shown in Fig. U1.2.2.

Once a separation of each series has been achieved by using the Hodrick–

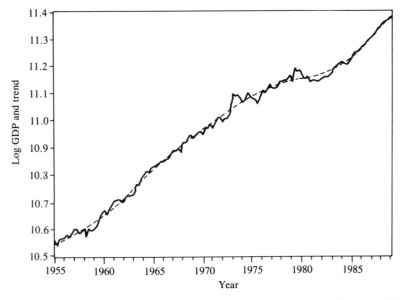

Figure U1.2.1 Actual (———) and trend (– – –) GDP using Hodrick–Prescott filters

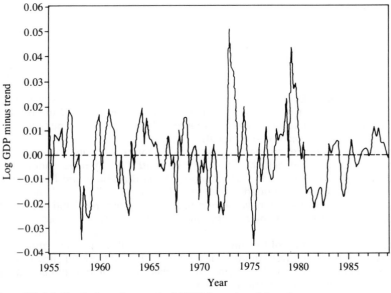

Figure U1.2.2 Deviations (———) of GDP from trend (– – –)

Table U1.2.1 Contemporaneous cross-correlations of business cycle components of macroeconomic time series with output

Expenditure variables	
Consumption	0.68
Investment	0.74
Exports	0.49
Imports	0.56
Production input variables	
Employment	0.38
Hours per worker	0.49
Real wage	0.24
Labour productivity	0.12
Monetary variables	
M1 money supply	0.33
M3 money supply	0.14
Price level	-0.56

Prescott filter it is straightforward to examine the relationships between the cyclical components of each of the series considered. For example, Blackburn and Ravn estimate the set of contemporaneous cross-correlations as shown by Table U1.2.1.

In general, these correlations are consistent with the traditional story of the business cycle presented in many textbooks. The various components of aggregate expenditure are all closely positively correlated with the business cycle and, to a somewhat lesser extent, so are the various measures of labour input. However, the most surprising feature of these results is the *negative* correlation of the price level with the output cycle. This runs counter to most stories of the business cycle as being the result of aggregate demand shocks, and has been used by Kydland and Prescott as supporting evidence for their Real Business Cycle interpretaton of economic fluctuations.

Notes

1. Harvey (1985) describes models of this kind as *structural time-series models*. He also presents estimates of this type of model under specific assumptions about the processes generating the trend and cyclical components.
2. In its strictest sense, stationarity requires *all* the moments of the distribution of the variable in question to be constant. If we restrict attention to the mean and variance only then our definition is that of *covariance* or *weak sense* stationarity. In practice, most of the literature on time series omits these qualifiers and we will do likewise.
3. In order to make such a statement a statistical methodology must exist by which the two types of process can be tested against each other. The framework adopted by NP, and now widespread in applied economic research, is that of testing for a unit root in the series using

the test statistics put forward by Dickey and Fuller in a series of papers. The usual test statistic is the 't-ratio' on ρ in the following regression:

$$\Delta y_t = \rho y_{t-1} + \phi t + \sum_{i=1}^{l} \gamma_i \Delta y_{t-i} + \varepsilon_t$$

where l is large enough to ensure that ε is white noise, i.e. purely random. The main problem is that ρ does not follow the standard t-distribution, so we must rely on critical values determined via Monte Carlo methods. These are somewhat larger than those from the t-distribution with a 95 per cent critical value for a sample size 100 of around -3.49.

A thorough review of these methods would take us too far into the realms of econometrics for a textbook on macroeconomics, but the interested reader should read Mills (1990) for further discussion.

4. Business cycles can also result from changes in the tastes of households between consumption and leisure, but this would imply a pattern of comovement among the endogenous variables which is not seen in practice (cf. Plosser, 1989, and Chapter 4 for a more extended discussion).

Appendix: Solving difference equations

Difference equations have become an extremely important mathematical tool in economics generally and macroeconomics in particular. This reflects the increasing concern within the subject for modelling the motion of the economy through time rather than just its short-run equilibrium position at a point in time. Methods for solving difference equations are therefore an indispensable part of any macroeconomist's tool-kit of techniques. The purpose of this appendix is to review some simple solution techniques for difference equation models and to show the types of behaviour which can arise within these models.

Model 1: The linear first-order difference equation

A first-order difference equation in a variable x takes the form:

$$x_t = \beta_0 + \beta_1 x_{t-1} \qquad (A1.1)$$

Formally, this is referred to as a non-homogenous difference equation because of the inclusion of the constant term β_0. However, such an equation can always be transformed into an homogenous equation (i.e. one without a constant term) in the following manner. First, let us consider what the solution to the above equation would be if x was constant through time. This yields

$$\bar{x} = \beta_0/(1 - \beta_1) \qquad (A1.2)$$

This can be thought of as the equilibrium, or long-run, solution to the difference equation, i.e. that value of x which will be attained if x converges on a constant value over a long period of time. Using this expression, and subtracting β_0 from both sides, we obtain:

$$x_t^* = \beta_1 x_{t-1}^* \qquad (A1.3)$$

i.e. a first-order difference equation in x^* where $x_{t-i}^* = x_{t-i} - \bar{x}$.

The solution to an homogenous difference equation is obtained in the following manner. First, let us try the following expression to see if it will do as a solution:

$$x_t^* = A\lambda^t \qquad (A1.4)$$

Substituting into Eq. (A1.3) we obtain:

$$A\lambda^t = \beta_1 A \lambda^{t-1} \qquad (A1.5)$$

This equation is satisfied for any non-zero constant A providing that $\lambda = \beta_1$. Thus our solution to the difference equation can be written in the form:

$$x_t = \bar{x} + A\beta_1^t \qquad (A1.6)$$

To determine the value of the arbitrary constant we need some additional information. This is usually in the form of knowledge of the value taken by x at some particular date. In the case when this date is at the beginning of the period the additional information needed is referred to as an initial condition. Suppose, for example, we know that the value taken by x at date 0 is x_0. From Eq. (A1.6) we know that $x_0 = \bar{x} + A$, hence we can substitute for the unknown constant and write the solution to our difference equation in the form:

$$x_t = \bar{x} + (x_0 - \bar{x})\beta_1^t \qquad (A1.7)$$

If β_1 is less than one in absolute value then it is easy to see that x_t converges on the equilibrium value $\bar{x}$ as t becomes large. Two types of convergence can occur, depending on whether β_1 is positive or negative. When β_1 is positive and less than one, convergence is said to be monotonic, since x_t progresses smoothly towards the equilibrium value $\bar{x}$. However, when β_1 is negative but greater than -1, x_t will oscillate around the equilibrium, with the oscillations becoming progressively smaller as time progresses.

Model 2: The linear second-order difference equation

The general form for the linear second-order difference equation can be written:

$$x_t = \beta_0 + \beta_1 x_{t-1} + \beta_2 x_{t-2} \qquad (A1.8)$$

Many of the steps involved in solving an equation of this type are analogous to those needed to solve the first-order problem. The first step again involves solving for the long-run or equilibrium value of x, which this time yields:

$$\bar{x} = \beta_0/(1 - \beta_1 - \beta_2) \qquad (A1.9)$$

Equation (A1.8) can now be transformed into an homogenous equation by subtracting β_0 from both sides and rewriting as:

$$x_t^* = \beta_1 x_{t-1}^* + \beta_2 x_{t-2}^* \tag{A1.10}$$

where $x_{t-i}^* = x_{t-i} - \bar{x}$. Again, let us try $A\lambda^t$ as a solution. This time we obtain:

$$A\lambda^t = \beta_1 A\lambda^{t-1} + \beta_2 A\lambda^{t-2} \tag{A1.11}$$

Dividing both sides by $A\lambda^{t-2}$ yields a quadratic equation in λ with solutions:

$$\lambda_{1,2} = \frac{\beta_1 + \sqrt{\beta_1^2 + 4\beta_2}}{2} \tag{A1.12}$$

which, although somewhat more complicated than in the case of the first-order equation, can still be seen to depend on the parameters of the original difference equation.

From the above we may deduce that either $A_1 \lambda_1^t$ or $A_2 \lambda_2^t$ are acceptable as solutions to the difference equation (A1.8). Moreover, any linear combination of the two will also itself be a solution. A general solution can therefore be written as:

$$x_t = \bar{x} + A_1 \lambda_1^t + A_2 \lambda_2^t \tag{A1.13}$$

Because there are two arbitrary constants in this case (A_1 and A_2) we will need two pieces of prior information, or initial conditions, to eliminate these. For example, if we know x_0 and x_1 this would be sufficient.

The second-order equation is capable of generating a richer variety of behaviour than the first-order model. Suppose both λ_1 and λ_2 are real numbers, which will be true if $\beta_1^2 > 4\beta_2$. In this case both roots must be less than one in absolute value for stability or convergence on a long-run equilibrium. More interest, however, arises when λ_1 and λ_2 are complex rather than real, which will be true if $\beta_1^2 < 4\beta_2$. In this case cycles naturally arise as x moves through time. Instability can still occur when there are complex roots, but even here we will observe cycles. It is just that these will diverge rather than converge on equilibrium.

When the roots of the quadratic equation are complex they can be written as a pair of complex conjugates, i.e. a pair of numbers of the form:

$$\lambda_1 = \delta_0 + \delta_1 i \qquad \lambda = \delta_0 - \delta_1 i \tag{A1.14}$$

where i is the square root of -1. In this case the condition for stability can be written:

$$\delta_0^2 + \delta_1^2 < 1 \tag{A1.15}$$

Complex roots in different equations are extremely important in the analysis of economic dynamics because they naturally give rise to cyclical or periodic behaviour in the variable concerned.

2.
The economics of long-term growth

2.1 The stylized facts of growth

As in many areas of economics, growth theory begins with a set of stylized facts or phenomena to be explained. Theories are judged to be interesting only if they produce results which are in accordance with these facts. For our purposes the important features of the growth process which any theory must seek to explain are as follows:

1. In most economies real output per unit of labour grows at a roughly constant rate over long periods of time.
2. The stock of physical capital also grows at a roughly constant rate through time but its growth rate is higher than that of labour. Hence there is a tendency for the ratio of capital to labour to increase.
3. The growth rate of capital and real output are roughly the same in the very long run, though they can differ for substantial periods of time. There is therefore no clear trend in the ratio of capital to real output.

The plausibility of these hypotheses can be seen by examination of the long-run behaviour of labour productivity and the capital–output ratio as shown in Figs 2.1 and 2.2. Figure 2.1 shows output per employed worker over the period 1855–1988, and the graph is drawn on a log scale so the slope represents the percentage growth rate. We can see from this graph that the growth of labour productivity remains remarkably constant over the decades. There is some evidence of an increase in the proportional growth rate in the post-Second World War period, relative to the pre-1913 period. The variability of the series during the short inter-war period is too great to draw any firm conclusions about just where the change occurs. However, Fig. 2.1 certainly gives some justification for regarding the constancy of the underlying growth rate of labour productivity as a reasonable first approximation.

Let us now turn to the ratio of capital to real output as shown in Fig. 2.2.

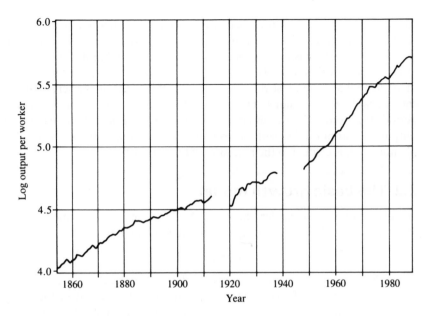

Figure 2.1 Output per employed worker: 1855–1988 (log scale)

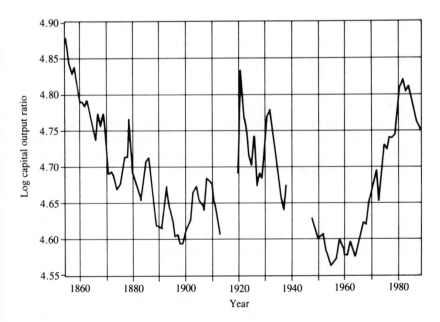

Figure 2.2 Ratio of capital to output: 1855–1988 (log scale)

The apparently greater variability of this series is mainly due to the much narrower scale on which the graph is drawn. However, it is obvious from this figure that there is no evidence of any long-run trend in this ratio. As an example of this, note that its value in 1870 is remarkably close to its value in 1979. Perhaps the most notable feature of this graph is the sensitivity of this variable to recessions. During the two downturns of the inter-war period, 1921 and 1931, we observe a sharp increase in the ratio of capital to output as output falls with a roughly stable capital stock. A similar phenomenon is evident in the recession of the early 1980s.

2.2 The basic growth model

In this section we consider the basic Neo-Classical growth model. Our starting point is the simple aggregate production function:

$$Y = F(N,K) \tag{2.1}$$

where Y is national output, N is input of labour services and K is input of capital services. This function is assumed to be well behaved in the sense that it has the standard Neo-Classical properties that the marginal products of both labour and capital are positive, but fall as the input of the factor concerned increases. Thus the first partial derivatives of Eq. (2.1) are positive but the second-order partial derivatives are negative. For our first look at this model we make two additional assumptions—that there is (1) no depreciation of capital and (2) no technical progress. Both these assumptions will be relaxed in later sections, where it will be shown that they do not qualitatively alter the results of the model.

Analysis is made considerably easier if we make use of a constant returns to scale assumption. This implies that a simultaneous increase of both factors of production, by a given percentage amount, will produce the same percentage increase in output. In mathematical terms, the function is said to be homogeneous of degree one. Using this assumption enables the production function to be written in per capita terms as:

$$y = f(k) \tag{2.2}$$

where $y = Y/N$ and $k = K/N$. The first derivative of Eq. (2.2) is positive since an increase in the capital–labour ratio increases per capita output, while the second derivative is negative, indicating that an increase in the amount of capital applied to a given labour force will have diminishing effects on per capita output.

Since technology is assumed to be constant, the only source of growth in this economy is through increases in one or both of the factors of production. Here we need to point out a basic difference in the nature of the two factors.

While the labour force is essentially exogenous to economic decisions, in that its growth depends mainly on demographic factors, capital is a produced factor, the availability of which depends on the economic decisions taken by agents within the economy. The ultimate external source of growth in the economy is therefore growth in the availability of labour. We assume that the labour force is growing through time at a constant proportional rate, n.

Our first task in analysing the growth process is to specify what the equilibrium growth path will look like. The term 'equilibrium' should not be taken to mean an unchanging position, since the growth process necessarily involves dynamic motion through time. Hence the literature on growth often makes use of the alternative terminology *steady-state growth path*. Given the assumption of no technical progress, the steady-state growth path must be one in which the level of income per capita and capital intensity are constant. We will use this as a basis for defining the nature of the growth path.

First, consider the rate of change of the level of capital intensity, k. This can easily be shown to equal the difference between the rate of growth of capital services, K, and the rate of growth of the labour supply, N. This is shown by

$$\frac{\dot{k}}{k} = \frac{\dot{K}}{K} - \frac{\dot{N}}{N} = \frac{\dot{K}}{K} - n \qquad (2.3)$$

where a dot above a variable indicates its derivative with respect to time.

Multiplying through by the level of capital intensity yields an equation of the form below, which states that the change in capital intensity with respect to time is equal to the difference between investment per capita and the growth rate of the labour force multiplied by the level of capital intensity. The latter term tells us the amount of additional capital necessary to maintain capital intensity at its existing level as the labour force grows through time.

$$\dot{k} = \frac{\dot{K}}{N} - nk \qquad (2.4)$$

Now through the standard national income accounting identities we know that the level of investment per capita must be equal to the level of saving per capita. If we make the additional assumption that the marginal propensity to consume is a constant then we can make use of the per capita production function to rewrite Eq. (2.4) as:

$$\dot{k} = sf(k) - nk \qquad (2.5)$$

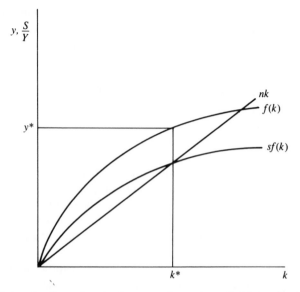

Figure 2.3 Determination of output per capita and capital intensity in the Neo-Classical growth model without technical progress

This equation plays a very prominent role in growth theory and is referred to as the *fundamental equation of Neo-Classical growth theory*. It states that the level of capital intensity will be increasing (or decreasing) through time if the level of savings per capita is greater (or smaller) than the amount needed to equip the new entrants to the labour force with the same amount of capital as those already employed.

Equation (2.5) also gives us a basis for the determination of the steady-state rate of growth. We have already argued that this will be achieved when the capital–labour ratio is constant through time. From Eq. (2.5) we see that this is achieved when $sf(k) = nk$. Moreover since k is constant this implies that K, the capital stock, must be growing at the same rate as N, the labour supply, and, given the assumption of constant returns to scale, output (Y) must also be growing at the same rate. Hence in the steady-state output, capital and labour all grow at the same constant proportional rate (n), which is given by the exogenous rate of growth at the labour supply.

The characteristics of the steady-state growth path can be most easily illustrated by the use of a diagram. Figure 2.3 illustrates some of the important features of the analysis we have been developing. On the horizontal axis there is the level of capital intensity. The two curved lines $f(k)$ and $sf(k)$ show the output and savings per capita, respectively, and the straight line shows the amount of per capita output necessary to maintain

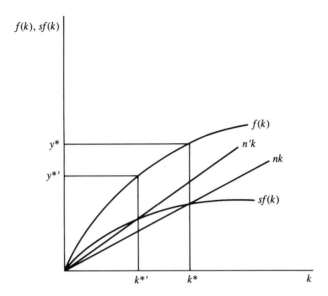

Figure 2.4 Effects of an increase in labour force growth

the level of capital intensity. The intersection of the $sf(k)$ and nk lines determines the level of capital intensity at which the economy is on the steady-state growth path k^*. This in turn determines the steady-state level of output per capita y^*, which is constant because of the absence of technical progress.

The diagrammatic approach can also be used to illustrate the factors which may act to change the nature of the steady-state growth path. Let us first consider an increase in the exogenously given growth rate of the labour force. This shifts the position of the nk line to $n'k$, as shown in Fig. 2.4, where n' is the new rate of labour growth. The new steady state has some surprising features. Although the rate of growth of output is now higher, the level of output per capita is now lower than on the original steady-state growth path. In explaining this result we must look at what has happened to the level of capital intensity.

Because there is now a faster growth rate in the labour supply a greater fraction of resources must now be devoted simply to equipping the new labour with the existing level of capital possessed by the workers already employed. This is what is represented by the upward rotation of the nk line to $n'k$. Since savings per capita are determined according to a stable function of the capital–labour ratio this in turn implies that the level of capital intensity which can be sustained ($k^{*'}$) falls. Finally, it can be seen from the per capita production function that the level of output per capita

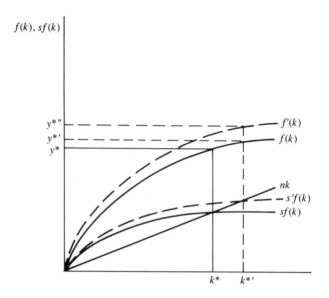

$f(k), sf(k)$

$y^{*''}$
$y^{*'}$
y^*

$f'(k)$
$f(k)$

nk
$s'f(k)$
$sf(k)$

k^* $k^{*'}$

Figure 2.5 Effects of an increase in savings ratio or step increase in productivity

($y^{*'}$) along the new steady-state growth path must also be lower. An increase in the growth rate of the labour force therefore has rather undesirable effects in terms of economic welfare since, despite the fact that the growth rate of the economy increases, the level of output per capita, and hence the welfare of the individual worker within the economy, necessarily falls.

Now let us consider the effects on the steady-state growth path of a shift upwards of the per capita savings function. This is illustrated by a movement of the savings function to a new position $s'f(k)$ in Fig. 2.5. Such a shift can come about for one of two reasons. The first of these is an increase in the marginal propensity to save and the second is a one-off increase in the level of total factor productivity. While both produce the same effect on the per capita savings function, the effect on the per capita production function is to leave it constant, in the case of an increase in the savings ratio, and to shift it upwards to $f'(k)$, in the case of a productivity improvement. In terms of the effect on the steady-state growth path we can see that either effect will shift the intersection with the nk line to a higher level of capital intensity $k^{*'}$ and will therefore increase the steady-state level of output per capita to $y^{*'}$. However, in the case where an increase in total factor productivity is responsible for the increase in per capita savings, the per capita production function itself shifts, leading to a further increase in output per capita to $y^{*''}$. Note that in both these cases the steady-state growth rate remains constant at n.

2.3 Depreciation and technical progress

The purpose of this section is to relax two of the assumptions we made in our account of the basic growth model and to show that these alter the conclusions of that account only very slightly. The two assumptions we deal with are those of zero depreciation of capital and zero technical progress.

Turning first to the depreciation of capital, we will modify our assumption of zero depreciation by allowing a fixed proportion of the capital stock to become redundant within each time period. This implies that savings and net investment are no longer identical, since part of the flow of savings must go to replace the capital that is worn out during the production process. Thus the growth of the capital stock through time must now be expressed as

$$\dot{K} = S - \lambda K \qquad (2.6)$$

where λ is the rate of depreciation of capital, i.e. the fraction of the stock of capital which is worn out within a single time period. To see the effects of this on the growth model we substitute Eq. (2.6) into Eq. (2.4) to obtain a new version of the fundamental equation of the form:

$$\dot{k} = sf(k) - (n + \lambda)k \qquad (2.7)$$

The only difference between this version of the fundamental equation and the one we derived in our account of the basic growth model is that the rate of depreciation of capital affects the amount of total savings which must be set aside for the maintenance of the level of capital intensity. This is intuitively obvious, since it is now no longer just the growth in the labour supply which requires the setting aside of some part of savings for this purpose but also the fact that part of the existing capital stock is worn out through use.

In terms of its effect on the steady-state growth path, the effect of capital depreciation is to reduce the steady-state capital–labour ratio and output per capita level. However, the steady-state growth rate itself remains unchanged at the natural level, n. In diagrammatic terms an increase in the rate of depreciation would produce an effect exactly the same as that illustrated in Fig. 2.4.

The existence of technical progress involves rather more substantial changes to the basic model. Let us begin with the form that technical progress might take. Two approaches have been suggested. In the first, disembodied technical progress, it appears as an exogenous improvement in the productivity of one or both of the factors of production. In the second, embodied technical progress, it can only occur through the installation of new capital with superior performance to the existing capital stock. While embodied technical progress is intuitively closer to the way in which we normally think of new technology impacting on the economy, it is analytically considerably harder to deal with. We are therefore going to concentrate on the rather more tractable case of disembodied technical progress. Moreover, again for reasons of analytical tractability, we are going to assume that technical progress takes the form of exogenous improvements in the productivity of labour. This form of technical progress is referred to as Harrod Neutral, and requires the modification of the aggregate production function along the following lines:

$$Y = F(A(t)N,K) \qquad (2.8)$$

where $A(t)$ is a positive function of time. Let us suppose that increases in labour productivity increase exponentially with a growth rate equal to γ. This implies that the $A(t)$ function takes the form $A(t) = A_0 e^{\gamma t}$.

The easiest way to analyse the model with technical progress is to redefine the per capita production function to be in terms of efficiency units of labour rather than simply the level of labour input. Measuring labour in terms of efficiency units means allowing for the fact that each hour of labour input will permit an increasingly larger rise in the level of output as time progresses because of the exogenous labour augmenting technical progress. In mathematical terms, this means dividing Y and K by $N_t A_0 e^{\gamma t}$ rather than by N_t to obtain a function of the form $\bar{y} = f(\bar{k})$, where a bar above a variable indicates that it is expressed in efficiency units.

We can now solve for the steady-state growth path in exactly the same way as we did in the basic growth model. First, we derive a new version of the fundamental equation written in terms of efficiency units:

$$\dot{\bar{k}} = sf(\bar{k}) - (n + \gamma)\bar{k} \qquad (2.9)$$

The steady state is achieved when the time derivative on the left-hand side of the equation is zero, i.e. when $sf(\bar{k}) = (n + \gamma)\bar{k}$. Again, this enables us to solve for the steady-state capital–labour ratio in efficiency units in the conventional manner.

The interesting feature of the growth model with technical progress is the effect it has on the steady-state growth rates of the three variables of interest—labour, capital and output. The growth rate of labour is still exogenously set at n, but those of capital and output now depend on the rate of technical progress. Since in steady state the capital–labour ratio in efficiency units is constant, this implies that capital must be growing at the same rate as efficiency units of labour. The growth rate of the latter is equal to the sum of the natural growth in labour supply (n) and the growth in labour productivity (γ). Hence the growth rate of capital equals $n + \gamma$. By a similar argument, the growth rate of output must also be equal to $n + \gamma$ since the level of output per efficiency unit of labour is constant in the steady state.

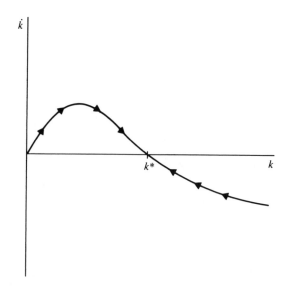

Figure 2.6 Dynamic adjustment of the capital–labour ratio

2.4 Dynamic adjustment, stability and the existence of the steady state

So far, we have concentrated exclusively on the properties of the steady state while neglecting the process by which the economy approaches this position. To rectify this, we will first present a simple account of the process by which the economy moves towards a steady-state position and then use this to discuss some problems about the stability and existence of such a state which were rather glossed over in the previous section.

To begin our discussion of the dynamic of growth let us first return to Fig. 2.3, which shows the determination of the steady-state level of capital intensity within the basic growth model. What happens when the capital–labour ratio is not at the stable level k^*? If it falls below k^* then savings per capita exceed the required level needed to maintain the existing level of capital intensity. This can be seen by the fact that the value taken by the $sf(k)$ function exceeds the nk function in Fig. 2.3. Therefore $\dot{k}$ is positive to the left of k^*. When $k > k^*$ then the opposite holds in that savings are insufficient to maintain the existing level of k and therefore the capital–labour ratio is falling. These observations can be used as the basis for the construction of a diagram showing the relationship between $\dot{k}$ and k as shown in Fig. 2.6. Providing the production function is well behaved as shown in Fig. 2.3 then the arrows of motion, which illustrate the motion of the economy through time, point towards the steady-state

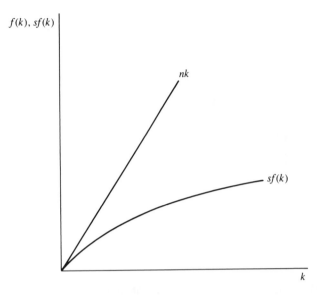

Figure 2.7 Non-existence of equilibrium when savings rate is too low

capital–labour ratio and the economy duly converges on it, given enough time.

The dynamic adjustment process illustrated in Fig. 2.6 also shows that the growth rate of output can deviate from the natural rate during the transition from one steady-state growth path to another. Consider, for example, the case of an increase in the marginal propensity to save which acts to increase the sustainable level of capital intensity. Immediately after such a change the economy will have a level of k which is below its steady-state value. This means that $\dot{k}$ will be positive and therefore capital will be growing faster than labour. It follows from the production function that the growth rate of output is also greater than the natural rate. The reverse argument holds for changes which reduce the steady-state value of k, in that growth will be below the natural rate during the transition period.

The version of the growth model discussed so far has assumed a production function which is sufficiently well behaved to guarantee the existence of a stable steady-state equilibrium growth path. Before leaving the model, however, it is useful to discuss two cases in which the production function does not have these necessary properties. First, consider the case shown in Fig. 2.7. Here the production function, and hence the savings function, has the standard Neo-Classical property of positive but diminishing returns to individual factors. However, the derivative of the per capita savings function is so low at all values of k that it fails to intersect with the nk line at a

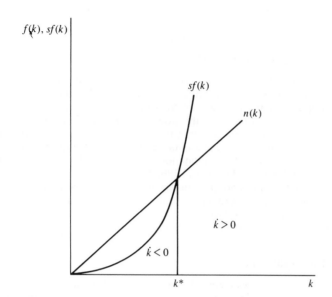

Figure 2.8 Instability with increasing returns

positive value of k. In this case the only stable steady state is one in which output per capita is zero, an unattractive result from both a theoretical and an empirical point of view. Thus we must modify our assumptions about the shape of the production function by including as an additional constraint that:

$$\lim_{k \to 0} sf'(k) > n \tag{2.10}$$

This is sufficient to ensure that the case shown in Fig. 2.7 does not occur.

Another possible problem arises if there are increasing returns to capital. This is illustrated in Fig. 2.8, which shows the case in which per capita output increases at an increasing rate with the level of capital intensity. The problem created in this case is that, although a steady-state capital–labour ratio exists, it is not stable. To the left of k^* savings per capita are lower than the demand for capital to maintain the existing level of capital intensity, while to the right of k^* savings are greater than the required level. This in turn implies that $\dot{k}$ is positive when $k > k^*$ and negative when $k < k^*$, thus the economy will tend to move cumulatively away from the steady-state growth path rather than towards it. This example illustrates the importance of the diminishing-returns assumption for the stability of the steady state.

Unit 2.1

Models of endogenous growth

The standard growth accounting procedure weights the inputs of labour and capital according to their shares in total income and takes the residual, obtained by subtracting the rate of growth of total factor input from total output, as an indicator of exogenous productivity growth. In the last few years a number of economists have begun to argue that this procedure is unsatisfactory, and that we should be modelling the determinants of productivity growth directly. This has led to the development of endogenous growth models which are particularly associated with the work of Romer (1986a,b).

The basic idea behind endogenous growth theory is that productivity growth should not be seen as an exogenous bonus for the economy but as something which is closely associated with the growth of the measured factor inputs. We will consider two cases where this may arise.

1. Knowledge spillovers

A natural question to ask is, why should the level of knowledge in the economy be positively related to its stock of capital? One possible justification for this is that capital growth is usually the result of the installation of new machinery which embodies the latest fruits of technological research. Once the capital is installed, this research effectively becomes public property, since everyone can observe and copy the innovation (subject to sufficient minor modifications to pacify the patent authorities). This in turn means that there is a spillover of knowledge every time a firm adds to its capital stock, i.e. the stock of knowledge is positively related to the capital stock. An interesting welfare property arises in this type of model in that the market outcome will be Pareto inefficient. Since firms cannot appropriate all the returns to investment in new technology they will tend to underinvest in both capital and basic research.

2. Specialized capital

The second approach to endogenous growth makes use of an idea which goes back to the Classical economists and, in particular, Adam Smith. Let us start by assuming that the extent to which capital contributes to production is not just a function of the amount of capital but the extent to which it is divided up into specialized units. As an example, think of an economy in which the capital stock consists of machine tools. The productivity of the capital stock will depend on whether these are general-purpose tools to be applied to all tasks or if they are divided up into a number of sub-groups tailored for specific production requirements. Thus, as the stock of capital increases, it becomes possible to achieve a higher level of specialization of capital goods, and this in turn makes it possible to achieve higher levels of labour productivity.

Both the cases described above would lead us to put rather more weight on the growth rate of capital than is standard in the literature on growth accounting. This is because in both cases, although for very different reasons, there are unmeasured externality effects associated with having a rapid growth in the capital stock. In practice, this means that a substantial fraction of the unexplained element in the growth accounting formula, i.e. the Solow Residual, would be attributed to capital growth rather than exogenous technological progress.

Unit 2.2

Classical models of the growth process

It is in modelling the growth process that the differences between the Classical economists and their Neo-Classical successors are most obvious. The Neo-Classical model treats the growth of the labour supply as exogenous and hence labour growth becomes the ultimate determinant of the steady-state growth rate (along with technological progress). In sharp contrast, the Classical economists made the endogeneity of the labour supply the main feature of their approach to explaining economic growth. This is particularly evident in the work of Thomas Malthus (1766–1834).

The key causal linkage in the Classical growth model is between the rate of population growth and the level of income per capita. Malthus's famous argument is that population will always expand up to the point at which income per capita is at subsistence level. If income is higher than subsistence then the death rate falls, because of higher nutritional standards, and the birth rate rises as people choose to have more children. The higher population which results means that the labour force expands, and output per capita falls, because of the existence of diminishing returns. This process continues until the level of output per capita has been driven down to a level where, once again, the birth and death rates for the economy are consistent with a stable population.

It is interesting to consider how the Classical growth model responds to the kind of exogenous disturbance we considered in the case of the Neo-Classical model. Consider, for example, a one-off increase in labour productivity due to some technological innovation. The immediate effect is for income per capita and living standards to rise. However, this then sets in motion the kind of Malthusian dynamics we described in the previous paragraph. Population starts to rise and income to fall until equilibrium is restored at the subsistence level of income per capita, albeit with a higher level of population than previously. This process is illustrated in Fig. U2.2.1, which shows the relationship between labour force growth on the vertical axis and the level of output per capita on the horizontal axis. The locus is upward sloping because of the linkages between the birth and death rates and the standard of living. A one-off increase in labour productivity moves the economy from the subsistence level A to position B. At B, population growth is positive but labour productivity is now falling. The economy therefore moves in the direction marked by the arrows back to the subsistence level of income.

What is noticeable about the Classical growth model is that growth is not viewed as a permanent or steady-state feature of the economy. Economic growth occurs during the transition from one equilibrium population level to another. It is little wonder that economics was dubbed the 'dismal science' in the days of the Classical economists, since this type of model allows for no possibility of improving living standards in the long run.

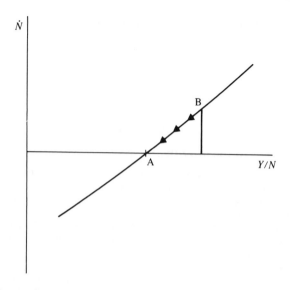

Figure U2.2.1 Reaction to productivity shock in the classical growth model

Review questions

1. Suppose the economy is characterized by a Cobb–Douglas production function of the form:

$$Y = AK^{\alpha}N^{1-\alpha}$$

   (a) Show that the above function exhibits constant returns to scale.
   (b) Derive an expression for the marginal product of labour and show that it is increasing with respect to the capital–labour ratio.

2. Using appropriate diagrams, illustrate and explain the effects of a reduction in the rate of growth of the labour force on the growth rate and level of output per capita.

3. Consider an economy with a Cobb–Douglas production function $Y = \sqrt{KN}$ productivity growth equal to 2 per cent per annum, a marginal propensity to consume equal to 0.8 and a growth rate of labour equal to 3 per cent per annum.

   (a) Compute the steady-state growth rate of output.
   (b) Compute the steady-state growth rate of output per capita.
   (c) Compute the steady-state capital–labour ratio.

4. Suppose the economy is characterized by a Cobb–Douglas production function of the form:

$$Y = K^{0.4}N^{0.6}$$

(a) Derive an expression for the level of output per capita.
(b) Given that the marginal propensity to consume is 0.8, there is no technical progress and the rate of growth of the labour force equals 3 per cent per annum, calculate the steady-state capital–labour ratio.

5. The table below gives data on growth rates of GDP for the four largest EC economies. Try plotting the growth rate for each of the countries in turn in order to identify major turning points in the growth pattern.

GDP at market prices

	Germany	France	Italy	UK
1961	4.6	5.5	8.2	3.3
1962	4.7	6.7	6.2	1.0
1963	2.8	5.3	5.6	4.2
1964	6.7	6.5	2.8	5.1
1965	5:5	4.8	3.3	2.3
1966	2.9	5.2	6.0	1.9
1967	−0.1	4.7	7.2	2.8
1968	5.6	4.3	6.5	4.1
1969	7.5	7.0	6.1	0.8
1970	5.1	5.7	5.3	2.9
1971	2.9	5.4	1.6	2.7
1972	4.2	5.9	3.2	2.3
1973	4.7	5.4	7.0	7.7
1974	0.3	3.2	4.1	−1.0
1975	−1.6	0.2	−3.6	−0.6
1976	5.4	5.0	5.9	3.8
1977	3.0	4.6	1.9	1.1
1978	2.9	3.4	2.7	3.6
1979	4.2	3.2	4.9	2.1
1980	1.4	1.6	3.9	−2.1
1981	0.2	1.2	1.1	−1.2
1982	−0.6	2.5	0.2	1.1
1983	1.5	0.7	0.5	3.5
1984	2.8	1.4	3.5	2.0
1985	2.1	1.7	2.7	3.7
1986	2.6	2.1	2.7	2.9
1987	1.6	2.2	3.1	3.6
1988	2.1	2.3	3.1	3.1

Source: Eurostat

3.
The Neo-Classical macroeconomic model

3.1 Core assumptions of the Neo-Classical model

In this chapter we examine the Neo-Classical macroeconomic model. The core assumptions of this model can be stated quite simply:

1. Agents are rational individuals who maximize utility subject to the constraints with which they are faced.
2. The market mechanism acts to coordinate the actions of individual agents through the price mechanism, i.e. prices are set so as to bring demand and supply into equality within each market.

A third assumption is normally added:

3. Agents have perfect information on all prices in all markets.

More modern theorists in the Neo-Classical tradition have relaxed this assumption while maintaining the first two. This modified analysis is termed *New Classical macroeconomics.*

The assumptions of rationality and market clearing are standard within microeconomic theory and, indeed, much of the material of this chapter will be familiar to readers from microeconomic courses. The main difference is that we are more interested in the general equilibrium properties of the system rather than behaviour within individual markets. To that end, we consider markets which are themselves broad aggregates of individual sub-markets, i.e. the goods, labour and money markets. While we must devote some time to looking at the operation of each of these broad groups in isolation, we are mainly interested in the interaction between them.

The models in this chapter are best described as Neo-Classical, rather than simply Classical. Why is it necessary to make this distinction? The problem lies with Keynes's indiscriminate use of the term 'Classical economics' to cover the work of just about all economists prior to himself. In fact, the orthodoxy Keynes saw himself attacking was that of Neo-Classical economics in that it assumes that demands and supplies are determined according to marginalist principles. This style of analysis originated in the late nineteenth and early twentieth centuries, and can be seen as a progression from the earlier Classical economists such as Smith, Ricardo and Marx. In this book we reserve the term 'Classical' to describe economists writing in the pre-marginalist tradition and who are, in general, concerned with issues other than those of the Neo-Classicists. Classical political economy in the tradition of Smith and Ricardo is concerned with dynamic questions of growth, production and distribution. Neo-Classical economics, at least that current at the time of Keynes, is concerned with static questions of exchange and welfare. While more dynamic models have since been constructed using the Neo-Classical methodology, it is important to maintain the distinction between the Neo-Classical and Classical modes of analysis.

3.2 Individual markets within the Neo-Classical system

There are three important markets to be considered: the labour market, the market for loanable funds and the money market. We will examine each in turn, specifying the determinants of demand and supply and the mechanism by which equilibrium is brought about.

Consider first the labour market. We assume the existence of a well-behaved production function of the form:

$$Y = F(N,K,\phi_1) \qquad (3.1)$$

where $F_N > 0, F_K > 0, F_{\phi_1} > 0, F_{NN} < 0$ and $F_{KK} < 0$. Y is net output, N and K are inputs of labour and capital, respectively, and ϕ_1 is a shift parameter which captures changes in productivity or, alternatively, changes in output which are not the result of changes in inputs of factors of production. The function is said to be well behaved since the marginal products of both labour and capital increase as inputs of each factor rise, but the rate of increase declines as more of each factor is applied for a given input of the other factor. In other words, we have diminishing returns to both labour and capital. While it is not essential to anything in the model, it is often convenient to make the additional assumption that there are constant returns to scale for simultaneous increases in both labour and capital, i.e.

$$F(\lambda N, \lambda K, \phi_1) = \lambda Y \qquad (3.2)$$

Unless stated otherwise, we will maintain the assumption that the economy can be characterized in terms of an aggregate production function of this type throughout this chapter. In addition, since we are concerned with the short-run equilibrium of the economy, we will also assume that the stock of capital is fixed. This implies that the equilibrium is defined over a period of time during which the investment which takes place does not accumulate sufficiently to make a significant difference to the overall level of the capital stock.

Under the assumptions relating to the shape of the aggregate production function described above, the profit-maximizing demand for labour is determined by the equality of the real wage rate and the marginal product of labour, or the partial derivative of F with respect to N. Thus the demand curve is of the form:

$$N^d = N^d(W/P, \bar{K}, \phi_1) \qquad (3.3)$$
$$N^d_{W/P} < 0, \qquad N^d_{\bar{K}} > 0, \qquad N^d_{\phi_1} > 0$$

The labour demand curve is therefore downward sloping with respect to the real wage rate and its position is determined by the inherited level of the capital stock and the value taken by the technological shift parameter θ_1.

We now turn to the derivation of the labour supply curve. This is determined via the optimizing choice between income and leisure for a representative household. It is well known that the effect on labour supply of an increase in real wages is ambiguous if income is an inferior good, since the substitution and income effects work in opposite directions. However, if we assume that either income is a normal good or that the substitution effect dominates any negative income effect, then we can write the labour supply curve as:

$$N^s = N^s(W/P, A, \phi_2) \qquad (3.4)$$
$$N^s_{W/P} > 0, \qquad N^s_A < 0, \qquad N_{\phi_2} > 0$$

A represents non-labour income, which we would normally expect to consist of interest and capital gains accruing to holdings of financial assets. In practice, this term is frequently neglected in simple expositions of the Neo-Classical model and we shall omit it for the rest of this chapter. ϕ_2 is a shift parameter included to capture exogenous changes in the tastes of households between income and leisure. An increase in ϕ_2 implies a shift in preferences towards income and away from leisure.

Figure 3.1 puts the labour demand and supply curves together to illustrate the determination of equilibrium in the labour market. For given values of capital, private sector financial assets, the level of technology and household tastes there is a unique combination of the real wage and the level of employment which yields labour market equilibrium. Since output is determined by the aggregate production function, this equilibrium also determines the level of output for the economy. Figure 3.1 also illustrates the comparative static effects of changes in the technology and taste shift

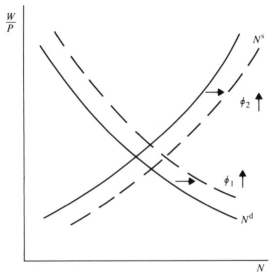

Figure 3.1 Comparative statics of the Neo-Classical labour market

parameters. An improvement in technology increases both the real wage and employment by shifting the demand curve outwards. This obviously also implies an increase in the level of output. A shift in household preferences towards income leads to an increase in employment and output but a fall in the real wage.

The second important market we consider is that for loanable funds. It is in this market that the levels of saving, investment and the rate of interest are determined. Again, the model is specified in terms of a demand and a supply side. Consider first the demand for loanable funds. This reflects the desire of firms to add to the capital stock—in other words, to undertake investment. Using either the net present value or the internal rate of return approach, economic theory predicts a negative impact of the rate of interest on the optimum capital stock. Since investment constitutes the incremental demand for capital we therefore also expect a downward-sloping relationship between investment and the rate of interest. On the supply side of the market the flow of loanable funds made available to firms depends on the choice of households between current and future consumption, with the rate of interest constituting the relative price of the two. Theory does not enable us to derive unambiguously the way in which an increase in the rate of interest affects current consumption and savings, since there are offsetting income and substitution effects. However, if we assume that the substitution effect dominates, then we get the intuitively appealing result that a rise in the rate of interest produces an increase in savings, and hence the supply of loanable funds.

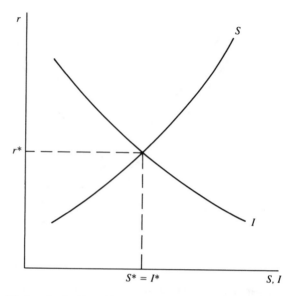

Figure 3.2 Equilibrium in the Neo-Classical model of the loanable funds market

Putting the demand and supply sides of the loanable funds market together determines the equilibrium rate of interest and levels of savings and investment. This is illustrated in Fig. 3.2. This account of the determination of savings and investment may seem radically different to the Keynesian model in that it appears to give no role to the level of income. Although income does not appear explicitly in our account of this market, it is, nevertheless, an important determinant of savings and investment. However, its effect is more complex than in the Keynesian model. A lot depends on whether any change in income is expected to persist through time or is seen as purely temporary. This will be discussed in detail in Chapter 6, but the main effects can be stated as follows. A permanent increase in income will increase both savings and investment but a temporary increase will have little effect on either.

Finally, we turn to the money market. Money plays a very passive role in the Neo-Classical model. Since the level of output has already been determined by the equilibrium in the labour market, money does not affect the real side of the economy at all. Instead its role is simply to determine the overall level of prices. To understand the role of money within the Neo-Classical model we begin with Fisher's (1927) equation of exchange. This can be stated as:

$$MV = PT \tag{3.5}$$

where M is the exogenously determined stock of money, V is the velocity of circulation, P is the price level and T is the number of transactions which take place during a given period. This relationship constitutes an identity, since the velocity of circulation is defined in such a way that the relationship must always hold. However, it can be turned into a theory of the price level by making the following assumptions:

1. The velocity of circulation is determined by the structure of the banking system and is fixed, at least in the short run.
2. There is a fixed relationship between final income or output and the number of transactions taking place. This is equivalent to assuming that the relationship between final and intermediate transactions remains constant which in turn enables us to replace T by Y in Eq. (3.5).
3. The level of income, Y, is determined in the labour market and hence can be regarded as fixed for the purposes of analysing the money market.

Incorporating these assumptons into the equation of exchange enables us to write an equation for the determination of the price level of the form:

$$P = [\bar{V}/\bar{Y}]M \tag{3.6}$$

Since the price level is a constant multiple of the money stock it follows that the rate of inflation is homogeneous of degree one in the rate of increase of the money stock.

3.3 The Neo-Classical model as a system

In Sec. 3.2 the individual sectors of the Neo-Classical model were discussed. In this section we consider the general equilibrium properties of the system, i.e. the ways in which the different markets interact with each other, and this interaction is illustrated in Fig. 3.3. The four panels of this diagram labelled (a), (b), (c) and (d) represent the labour market, the loanable funds market, the aggregate production function and the equation of exchange, respectively.

The relationship between the markets can be understood as follows. Equilibrium in the labour market determines the real wage rate and the volume of employment (panel (a)). This in turn determines the level of real output through the aggregate production function (panel (c)). For a given level of real income and nominal money stock the price level is determined in the money market (panel (d)). Finally, the interest rate, and the division of real income between consumption and savings/investment, is determined in the loanable funds market (panel (b)). In effect, the Neo-Classical system is *recursive*. Although equilibrium in the labour market influences the price level via the money market there is no feedback from the money market to

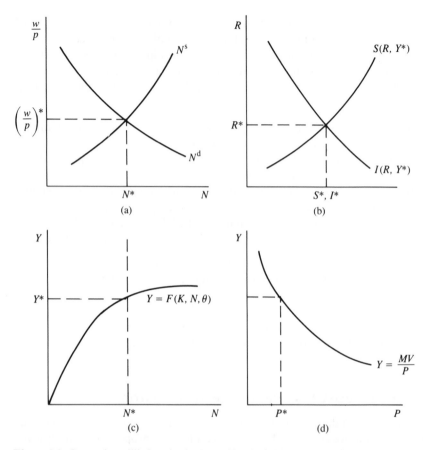

Figure 3.3 General equilibrium in the Neo-Classical macroeconomic model

the real sector of the economy. This is the basis of the hypothesis of the *neutrality of money*, i.e. the proposition that the money stock has no role other than the determination of the overall price level. It is easy to show using Fig. 3.3 that the comparative static effects of an increase in the money stock are to raise the price level but to leave real output, employment and the rate of interest unchanged.

We argued in the previous paragraph that money has no effect on real magnitudes within the Neo-Classical model. However, there are factors which can change real magnitudes within the system we have set up. The most fundamental influences on real quantities in the Neo-Classical model are the *tastes* of households, as reflected in their income–leisure choices and the *technology* available to firms which determines the position of the aggregate production function and the demand for labour curve. A shift in household preferences away from leisure to income, or an improvement in technology, will increase output and employment and reduce the price level. However, the effect on the rate of interest is uncertain, since savings will increase, because of higher equilibrium income, and investment will also increase if the rise in income is expected to be permanent.

One final comparative static experiment needs to be considered. What is the reaction of the model to an increase in the level of government expenditure? The answer is that this model must exhibit complete crowding out. Since the level of output is determined in the labour market, and we have not built in any mechanism through which government expenditure affects this market, there must be some offsetting force at work to prevent an overall excess demand for goods emerging. This, in fact, operates through the loanable funds market. An increase in government spending lowers the available supply of loanable funds by requisitioning part of the flow of savings. This has the effect of raising the rate of interest and exactly offsetting the increase in government expenditure by a cut in investment. Of course, this is likely to lead to adverse long-run supply side effects, but in the short run, during which the capital stock is fixed, output remains unaltered. Thus both the standard Keynesian tools of demand management are impotent within the Neo-Classical framework. The only factors affecting real output in the short run are the fundamental ones of tastes and technology.

3.4 A Neo-Classical approach to the business cycle

The static Neo-Classical model described above might appear unsuitable as a vehicle for explaining cyclical fluctuations in real output. However, with a few minor modifications it is possible to use it to formulate a simple business cycle model with many features in common with the real business cycle literature (RBC) surveyed by Plosser (1989).

We begin by adopting log-linear versions of the demand and supply for labour curves in which the technology and taste parameters enter additively:

$$n^d = -\alpha w/p + \phi_1 \qquad (3.7)$$

$$n^s = \beta w/p + \phi_2 \qquad (3.8)$$

Lower-case letters in the above equations indicate that we have expressed the variables in terms of deviations from their equilibrium values in order to simplify the notation. Now suppose that instead of interpreting the shift parameters in terms of once-and-for-all comparative static effects we specify them as stochastic variables, each following a normal distribution and which are uncorrelated with each other. Now if we solve Eqs (3.7) and (3.8) as a pair of simultaneous equations in employment and the real wage, it is straightforward to solve for the variances of the real wage and employment:

$$\text{var}(w/p) = \frac{1}{(\alpha + \beta)^2} [\text{var}(\phi_1) + \text{var}(\phi_2)] \qquad (3.9)$$

$$\text{var}(n) = \left[\frac{1 - \alpha}{\alpha + \beta}\right]^2 \text{var}(\phi_1) + \left[\frac{\alpha}{\alpha + \beta}\right]^2 \text{var}(\phi_2) \qquad (3.10)$$

(Recall that the variance of the sum of two random variables is the sum of their variances plus twice their covariance or, more generally:

$$\text{var}(ax + by) = a^2\text{var}(x) + b^2\text{var}(y) + 2ab\,\text{cov}(x,y)$$

The covariance term disappears in the equations reported here because the disturbances to the demand and supply curves are assumed to be uncorrelated with each other.)

However, the main source of interest here is the *covariance* between employment and the real wage rate. This can be derived as:

$$\text{cov}(n,w/p) = \frac{1}{(\alpha + \beta)^2} [\beta\text{var}(\phi_1) - \alpha\text{var}(\phi_2)] \qquad (3.11)$$

This covariance can be either positive or negative, depending on the slopes of the demand and supply curves and the variances of the tastes and technology disturbances. For a positive covariance we must have:

$$\text{var}(\phi_1) > \left[\frac{\alpha}{\beta}\right] \text{var}(\phi_2) \qquad (3.12)$$

i.e. the variance of the disturbance to technology must be greater than the variance of the disturbance to tastes multiplied by the ratio of the demand and supply elasticities of employment with respect to the real wage.

This is intuitively quite an appealing result. We have seen that technology disturbances raise both real wages and employment while taste disturbances raise employment but lower real wages. For employment and real wages to move together it must therefore be the case that technology disturbances are relatively more important than taste disturbances.

Now it is one of the well-known stylized facts of economics that the real wage and the level of employment both move pro-cyclically. This is illustrated by Fig. 3.4, which shows changes in the employment and the real wage rate over the period 1961–88. There is a clear (though not particularly strong) positive correlation between the two series. Therefore if we interpret the economy in the way described above we must logically conclude that productivity disturbances are more important than disturbances to tastes in generating economic fluctuations.

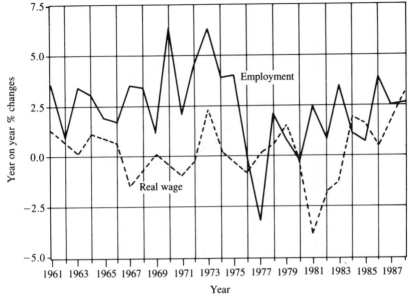

Figure 3.4 Changes in employment (———) and real wages (– – –), 1961–88

The model presented here captures some of the flavour of the RBC approach. It does not constitute a full RBC model since it maintains the unrealistic assumption of a fixed capital stock. Changes in the capital stock perform an important role in RBC models in that they generate persistence in output fluctuations. However, despite this caveat, the model has a good deal in common with RBC models in emphasizing the potential importance of productivity shocks in generating economic fluctuations. In addition, like RBC models, it is rooted firmly in the paradigm of market clearing and optimizing agents which characterizes Neo-Classical methodology.

3.5 The price-surprise model of output fluctuations

Another attempt to generate models which can explain fluctuations in employment and output, but which are consistent with Neo-Classical principles, has been provided by the work of Robert Lucas (1972) and various others. This body of work has concentrated on the importance of expectations in the determination of macroeconomic equilibrium and the possibility that mistakes in forming expectations can lead to short-term movements in the level of real output. The type of model put forward in this literature is therefore frequently referred to as a price-surprise model.

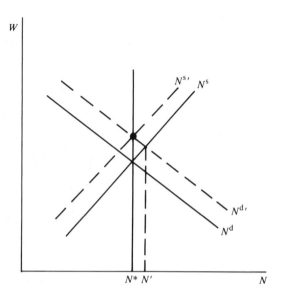

Figure 3.5 The Lucas price-surprise model

To explain the basic ideas of this literature we will adopt a graphical approach. Figure 3.5 shows a typical representation of a Neo-Classical labour market. The demand for labour curve is shown to be downward sloping on the assumption that there are diminishing returns to labour. The supply of labour curve is drawn as upward sloping on the assumption that any negative income effect on labour supply of a rise in wages is offset by a positive substitution effect. However, Fig. 3.5 is drawn with the nominal wage rather than the real wage on the vertical axis. Hence the position of both the curves shown depends upon the price level. The reason for this modification of the diagram will become obvious with the exposition of the model.

Let us consider the effects of an increase in the price level on the equilibrium of this economy. For any given nominal wage rate the demand for labour will rise since the marginal revenue product of labour has increased. This is shown by a shift of the labour demand curve to the broken line indicated by $N^{d'}$ in the figure. Simultaneously, the supply curve of labour will shift backwards as households realize that the real value of any given nominal wage rate has fallen. This is indicated by the shift of the labour supply curve to the broken line $N^{s'}$ in the figure. Since tastes and technology remain unchanged it must be the case that these shifts offset each other and leave the equilibrium level of employment unchanged at N^*.

Real effects of changes in prices can only come about if agents on one side or other of the market make mistakes in their estimates of the price level. This basic idea was introduced by Milton Friedman (1968) in his attack on the Phillips curve, and has since been adopted and expanded on by the New Classical economists. Let us suppose that the two sides of the labour market differ in their access to information about the price level. Firms can observe their own prices and hence know the real wage accurately. Thus when the price level changes the demand for labour curve shifts in the way indicated in Fig. 3.5. Households, on the other hand, do not have up-to-date information on the price level and must form expectations of it in order to estimate the level of real wages. For the moment, assume that the increase in the price level has come as a surprise to households. If this is the case, then the labour supply curve remains constant and the equilibrium level of employment is therefore detemined by the intersection of the new labour demand curve and the original labour supply curve. This implies an expansion of employment from N^* to N'. It is therefore the case that when an increase in the price level comes as a surprise to the household sector of the economy it can have real effects on the levels of output and employment.

We have said nothing so far about the way in which households form their expectations about the price level. Prior to the mid-1970s the standard assumption was that of *adaptive expectations*. This involves the adjustment of expectations according to observed past errors. Thus, for example, the expectation of the price level at date t could be written as the expectation at date $t - 1$ plus some fraction of the observed error at date $t - 1$ as shown by

$$p_t^e = p_{t-1}^e + (1 - \gamma)(p_{t-1} - p_{t-1}^e) \qquad (3.13)$$

There are, however, two main objections to this assumption. The first is that in an inflationary world, i.e. one in which the growth rate of prices is consistently positive, agents will continuously underpredict the price level. Even under a very basic assumption of common sense we would expect them to notice that their mistakes were all in the same direction and adjust their expectations-formation mechanism accordingly. A second related objection to the adaptive expectations model is that it unnecessarily, and severely, restricts the information set which agents are assumed to use in forming expectations. It is implicitly assumed that only past observed prices are deemed relevant in predicting current and future prices. This again seems counter to common sense. There are numerous factors which go to determine the overall price level and which agents can readily observe. Why should we therefore adopt a theory of expectations which prohibits agents from taking any of these factors into consideration?

During the mid-1970s the objections outlined in the above paragraph led the New Classical economists to abandon the assumption of adaptive expectations and to replace it with that of *rational expectations*. Expectations are said to be rational when agents use all available information to construct the most efficient forecast possible of the variable of interest. From a theoretical point of view this constitutes a considerable advance, since it allowed agents to take into account any information deemed relevant in the determination of expectations. However, there is more to rational expectations than a simple expansion of the information set. It is assumed that agents make use of the information they have in the most efficient way possible to generate forecasts. Moreover, information is not simply restricted to observations on potentially relevant variables but can also include any relevant economic theory which might be helpful in explaining the variable of interest.

The importance of rational expectations can be made clearer within the context of a simple model. We will consider a simplified version of the controversial Sargent–Wallace (1976) model of the economy. This is controversial because it gives rise to some very strong results and policy implications. Our interest in it here, however, arises because of the way it combines the Neo-Classical macroeconomic framework with the assumptions of imperfect information and rational expectations.

The basic model can be expressed by the following three equations:

$$y_t = y_n + \alpha(p_t - p_t^e) + \varepsilon_{1t} \tag{3.14}$$

$$p_t = m_t + \varepsilon_{2t} \tag{3.15}$$

$$m_t = -\delta(y_{t-1} - y_n) + \varepsilon_{3t} \tag{3.16}$$

ε_1, ε_2, ε_3 are random disturbance terms which, for simplicity, are assumed to be uncorrelated with each other.

The first equation is a price-surprise supply function. It expresses the conventional New Classical assumption that deviations of output around its natural level y_n are the result of mistakes in forecasting the price level and random shocks to aggregate supply ε_1. Equation (3.15) is a simplified quantity theory equation for the price level. It is assumed that prices adjust on a one-for-one basis with respect to the money stock. Note that the level of output has been omitted from this equation in the interests of maintaining analytical tractability. It could easily be included in the equation, but at the expense of a considerable increase in difficulty without changing any of the qualitative results. Finally, Eq. (3.16) represents a government monetary policy reaction function. It indicates that the government is attempting to stabilize the economy by reducing the money supply when output is above the natural rate and increasing it when output is below the natural rate.

However, information lags are assumed to prevent the government from responding immediately to the state of the economy, so there is a one-period lag in its response to the observed state of the economy.

If we combine Eqs (3.14) and (3.15) we obtain

$$y_t - y_n = \alpha(m_t - m_t^e) + \varepsilon_{1t} \tag{3.17}$$

This shows that deviations of output from its natural level are the result of unexpected changes in the money stock as well as random supply shocks. Thus the price-surprise model allows money to be non-neutral, when changes in money are unexpected. This differentiates it from both the standard Neo-Classical model and the real business cycle model which we have looked at in previous sections.

We have said nothing so far about the way in which expectations are formed. In the spirit of New Classical analysis we will assume rational expectations. This gives rise to a number of very interesting results. The first point to note is that since agents can observe the level of output in the previous period, and they know that the government responds in a systematic manner to the state of the economy, they will incorporate this information into their forecast of the money stock and, in turn, their forecast of the price level. The rational expectation of the money stock can easily be seen to be given by $m_t^e = -\delta(y_{t-1} - y_n)$ and the forecast error is therefore given by the sum of the random disturbances to the quantity equation and to the money stock, i.e. $(m_t - m_t^e) = \varepsilon_{2t} + \varepsilon_{3t}$. If we substitute this expression into Eq. (3.17) we obtain

$$y_t - y_n = \varepsilon_{1t} + \alpha(\varepsilon_{2t} + \varepsilon_{3t}) \tag{3.18}$$

This indicates that deviations of output from its natural level are determined by the three types of random disturbance which hit the economy. More important is what does not appear in Eq. (3.18). Despite the government's attempts to stabilize the economy, the systematic part of monetary policy plays no role in influencing the distribution of output around the natural level. Since the disturbance terms are uncorrelated with each other it is easy to derive the variance of output around the natural level as:

$$\text{var}(y_t - y_n) = \text{var}(\varepsilon_{1t}) + \alpha^2(\text{var}(\varepsilon_{2t}) + \text{var}(\varepsilon_{3t})) \tag{3.19}$$

Therefore the government's choice of stabilization parameter, δ, does not influence the variance of output around the natural level. In particular, even if the government decides not to try to stabilize the level of output at all, i.e. it sets $\delta = 0$, this will leave the variance of output unchanged. New Classical models of this type are said to exhibit the *policy neutrality property*. This means that systematic attempts to stabilize the economy are ineffective. However, there is one way in which the government can affect the distribution of output, which is by making its policy less predictable or increasing the variance of the ε_3 term. Under normal circumstances we would expect that the government would want to make the variance of output as small as possible, and therefore the best thing for it to do is to make its policy as predictable as possible. It is often argued by New Classical economists that the best way to do this is to set a fixed rate of growth for the money supply along the lines suggested by Milton Friedman. However, there is no particular reason why this should be the case, since any systematic monetary policy should be as good as any other in stabilizing output.

3.6 Comparisons with Classical and Keynesian models

The short-run Neo-Classical model presented in Secs 3.3 and 3.4 is really an invention of Keynes deriving from the General Theory. When Keynes wrote his book a well-developed Neo-Classical model could not be said to exist. Keynes took the basic building blocks of Sec. 3.3 and developed them into a complete system for the purposes of comparison with his own alternative system. Of course, his aim was not to present a Neo-Classical model for its own sake but to contrast it unfavourably with his own analysis. We will argue in Chapter 4 that he was only partially successful in this. The Keynesian model has a much better-developed framework for understanding the linkages between the real and the monetary sectors, but it leaves unanswered too many important questions about the sources of nominal rigidity in wages and/or prices, which are ultimately the source of Keynes's unemployment equilibrium.

When we turn to the comparison of the Neo-Classical model with the analysis of the Classical economists then the most interesting point of contrast arises in their differing treatments of the growth process. Neo-Classical growth theory is usually content to adopt the simplifying assumption that the rate of growth of labour supply is exogenous. It is usually implicit in this to argue that labour growth is determined primarily by population growth, which in turn is determined by a variety of sociological and cultural factors, but not closely linked to any economic variable. The Classical economists had a quite different vision. In their view, both labour supply and population growth were closely linked to the real wage. If real wages rise the population expands until the labour supply grows sufficiently to return wages to some baseline level. This view is stated in its strongest form in the case of the 'Malthusian Trap', where population always expands to the level at which workers are earning a bare subsistence wage, and in which famine and war provide the only ultimate checks on its growth (cf. Unit 2.2 for a more detailed discussion).

Neo-Classical economics has adopted the research strategy of deriving behavioural relationships on the assumption of rational utility-maximizing agents. Agents' actions are then coordinated through the price mechanism to produce a Pareto-efficient market solution. There is really no need for a distinction between micro- and macroeconomics within the Neo-Classical paradigm since macroeconomics simply constitutes a particular scheme of aggregation designed to highlight the interactions between broad categories of market. The fundamental determinants of output and employment within the Neo-Classical scheme are the technology available to firms and the tastes of households between income and leisure. Money's only role is to determine the overall price level and there is complete crowding out of government expenditure.

Despite Keynes's claim to have provided a more general paradigm which encompasses it, Neo-Classical macroeconomics has retained an identity separate from Keynesian macroeconomics. Many modern macroeconomists see themselves as operating within a largely Neo-Classical framework. The difference is that these economists are willing to relax the assumption that agents have access to perfect information on all prices in all markets. The New Classical macroeconomics results from combining the Neo-Classical principles of utility maximization and market clearing with the presence of imperfect information in some markets.

Unit 3.1

Testing the price-surprise model

In a number of empirical papers Robert Barro has sought to test the price-surprise model of output fluctuations. His starting point is the proposition that, if the price-surprise model is correct, then only unanticipated increases in the money stock should act to increase the level of output. If monetary increases are anticipated, then they will be used to revise upwards the rational expectation of the price level, while leaving output unchanged.

Barro attempts to test this hypothesis by adopting a two-stage procedure. First, he models the determination of expected changes in the money stock, by regressing the actual change on its own lagged values and a set of economic variables are considered to be relevant. He then uses the fitted values from this regression as his measure of anticipated money growth. In the second stage of the Barro procedure an output equation is estimated and used to test the hypothesis that it is only the unanticipated component of the monetary growth rate which is important.

A representative example of the Barro procedure is contained in his 1978 *Journal of Political Economy* paper. In this he uses annual data for the US economy over the period 1941–76. The following equation is estimated for the rate of growth of narrow money:

$$\Delta M_t = 0.082 + 0.41\Delta M_{t-1} + 0.21\Delta M_{t-2} + 0.072FED_t + 0.026U_{t-1}$$
$$\quad\quad (0.027)\ (0.14)\quad\quad (0.12)\quad\quad (0.016)\quad\quad (0.009)$$

$$\bar{R}^2 = 0.77 \quad\quad DW = 1.9 \quad\quad \hat{\sigma} = 0.015 \quad\quad\quad\quad (U3.1.1)$$

Standard errors are given in parentheses below the coefficients. In this equation *FED* is a measure of Federal government expenditure relative to 'normal', and therefore captures the need of the government to cover its deficit by issuing money, while *U* is a measure of the civilian unemployment rate which captures any discretionary response of monetary policy to the state of the business cycle. Apart from the second lag on money growth, all the variables are statistically significant at the 5 per cent level. The above equation is then used to generate estimates of anticipated and unanticipated monetary growth, by using the fitted values as estimates of anticipated money and the residuals as estimates of unanticipated money.

In the second stage Barro estimates a model for the determination of output of the form:

$$y_t = 2.95 + 1.04\Delta MR_t + 1.21\Delta MR_{t-1} + 0.44\Delta MR_{t-2} + 0.26\Delta MR_{t-3} +$$
$$\quad (0.04)\ (0.21)\quad\quad (0.22)\quad\quad (0.21)\quad\quad\quad (0.16)$$
$$\quad\quad\quad\quad\quad\quad 0.55MIL_t = 0.0354t \quad\quad\quad\quad\quad (U3.1.2)$$
$$\quad\quad\quad\quad\quad\quad (0.09)\quad\quad (0.0004)$$

$$\bar{R}^2 = 0.998 \quad\quad DW = 1.8 \quad\quad \hat{\sigma} = 0.016$$

where *y* is the log of real Gross National Product, ΔMR is unanticipated money, *MIL* is a variable included to take account of the effect on output of the drafting of employees into the armed forces and *t* is a time trend included to take account of the secular growth in the level of output. All the unanticipated money variables are strongly statistically significant, lending support to the hypothesis that unanticipated money influences real output.

The above equation does not, however, test the price-surprise model. In order to do this, Barro adopts two procedures. First, an alternative output equation is estimated, which substitutes actual money growth for unanticipated money growth. This is found to have rather worse statistical properties than the equation reported above, in that the standard error of the regression is higher and the Durbin–Watson statistic indicates the presence of serial correlation in the residuals. Second, a composite equation is estimated which includes both unanticipated money growth and actual money growth. Using this composite equation, an *F*-test indicates that the actual money growth variables are jointly insignificant, while the unanticipated money growth variables remain significant. The overall conclusion is therefore that unanticipated money is important in determining real output while predicted or anticipated money is not.

While the Barro evidence might at first seem convincing, it should be noted that a number of authors have found that these results are not robust. When the model is estimated using data for other countries, or over different time periods, or by using quarterly data, quite different results can emerge.

Unit 3.2

Price and output responses to changes in nominal income

One of the central questions of macroeconomics has always been to what extent changes in aggregate demand will result in changes in real output and to what extent they will simply be reflected in prices. In the early 1970s Robert Lucas proposed a theoretical model of this split, as shown by the price-surprise model discussed in the text. However, theories remain vacuous until they are confronted with empirical evidence, and Lucas has attempted to do just this with his own theory.

Lucas's empirical method is to use an ingenious mixture of time-series and cross-section data to examine the consistency of the predictions of the price-surprise model with real-world data. In order to examine his method, let us first remind ourselves of the basic principles of the price-surprise model. Agents with this model make mistakes in distinguishing relative price movements from movements in the overall level of prices. Hence, a general expansion of output can come about if there is an expansion of aggregate demand, because large numbers of agents within the economy believe relative prices to be moving in their favour when, in fact, it is simply the case that the general price level has risen. The question we need to ask ourselves, however, is, what fraction of any given observed increase in his or her price will a rational agent attribute to a change in relative price, and what fraction will be attributed to a change in overall prices? The answer depends on the extent to which relative and overall prices have exhibited a high degree of volatility in the past. If the overall price level has been subject to a high degree of random disturbance then it is likely that much of the observed increase in price will be attributed to this cause. If, however, relative prices have been relatively more variable then a large fraction of the increase in price will be assigned to it.

It is the theoretical property described above which is central to Lucas's empirical methodology. He takes data for a number of national economies with differing inflationary experiences which are then used to estimate equations of the form:

$$\Delta y_t = \beta_0 + \beta_1 \Delta x_t + \beta_2 \Delta y_{t-1} \qquad \text{(U3.2.1)}$$

This relates the change in the log of real GNP/GDP to the change in the log of nominal GNP/GDP and its own lagged value. The coefficient β_1 measures the instantaneous response of real output to shifts in nominal demand while the coefficient β_2 measures the degree of persistence in real output in response to aggregate demand shocks. In other words, a high value of β_2 means that a one-off shock to demand will continue to have an effect on real output for a long time after it has occurred. High levels of both coefficients indicate an economy in which aggregate demand has powerful effects on real output which persist for a long time.

The price-surprise model makes testable predictions about the relative size of the coefficients β_1 and β_2, depending on the past inflationary experience of the countries considered. For example, if inflation rates have been highly unstable in one particular country, agents within that country may attribute a large fraction of any observed change in price to changes in the overall price level, and hence, the response of real output to changes in aggregate demand (and the persistence of that response) will be low. By a similar argument, if we take a country in which the inflation rate has been quite stable then we would expect to find relatively high values of the two coefficients β_1 and β_2.

In practice, Lucas finds exactly the sort of pattern in the empirical results which his theory predicts. As an example, let us consider the results for two contrasting economies—the United States and Argentina. These differ noticeably in their inflationary experience in that the United States has historically had much lower and more stable rates of inflation than Argentina. When Eq. (U3.2.1) is estimated for these two countries, using annual data over the period 1953–67 Lucas obtains the following results:

United States
$$\Delta y_t = -0.049 + 0.910\Delta x_t + 0.887\Delta y_{t-1} \qquad R^2 = 0.945 \qquad \text{(U3.2.2)}$$
$$\qquad\qquad\quad (0.086) \qquad (0.070)$$

Argentina
$$\Delta y_t = -0.006 + 0.011\Delta x_t - 0.126\Delta y_{t-1} \qquad R^2 = 0.018 \qquad \text{(U3.2.3)}$$
$$\qquad\qquad\quad (0.070) \qquad (0.258)$$

Standard errors are given in parentheses below the coefficients.

The difference in performance between the two equations is remarkable. That for the United States has significant coefficients and a high degree of explanatory power, indicating that aggregate demand influences real output strongly. In contrast, the equation for Argentina has small, insignificant coefficients and a very low R^2, indicating very little role for aggregate demand in causing changes in real output. Thus the evidence appears to be broadly consistent with Lucas's price-surprise model.

Review questions

1. Suppose the economy has a production function of the form:

$$Y = A\sqrt{N}$$

   (a) Derive an expression for the demand for labour curve.
   (b) Show that the demand for labour curve can be written as linear in logarithms.
   (c) How would you characterize an exogenous increase in labour productivity using the above function?
2. Suppose the economy has a Lucas supply curve of the form:

$$y = y_n + 0.5(p - p^e)$$

   and an aggregate demand function of the form:
$$m - p = 0.5y$$

   (a) Calculate the effects on output and price of an unanticipated increase in the money stock.
   (b) Calculate the effects on output and price of an anticipated increase in the money stock.

3. Consider an economy with a Cobb–Douglas production function of the form:

$$Y = AK^{0.4}N^{0.6}$$

(a) Derive an expression for the labour demand curve.
(b) Illustrate the effects of an increase in the capital stock on the demand for labour using a diagram.
(c) How can you use the above function to represent real business cycle fluctuations?

4. Discuss the determination of general equilibrium in the Neo-Classical macroeconomic system using diagrams. Show that there is an effective separation of the real and monetary sectors in this model.

UK: Growth rates of GDP and employment

	GDP	Employment
1961	3.3	1.2
1962	1.0	0.7
1963	4.2	0.1
1964	5.1	1.1
1965	2.3	0.9
1966	1.9	0.6
1967	2.8	−1.5
1968	4.1	−0.7
1969	0.8	0.1
1970	2.9	−0.5
1971	2.7	−1.0
1972	2.3	−0.2
1973	7.7	2.3
1974	−1.0	0.3
1975	−0.6	−0.4
1976	3.8	−0.8
1977	1.1	0.1
1978	3.6	0.6
1979	2.1	1.5
1980	−2.1	−0.3
1981	−1.2	−3.9
1982	1.1	−1.8
1983	3.5	−1.2
1984	2.0	1.9
1985	3.7	1.6
1986	2.9	0.4
1987	3.6	1.9
1988	4.4	3.1

Source: Eurostat

5. The shape of the production function plays an important role in all macroeconomic models. One way we can investigate its short-term properties is to look at the relationship between changes in employment and changes in GDP. The table on p. 57 gives the percentage changes for both of these for the UK economy. Try plotting them on the same graph to assess the strength of the relationship.

4.
The Keynesian macroeconomic model

This chapter introduces Keynesian macroeconomic analysis. The approach taken is methodologically quite distinct from that of the Classical model. In the case of the Classical model each market was modelled using the standard tools of microeconomic analysis: agents decide on purchases and sales of goods or factors of production conditional on relative prices and initial endowments of commodities. The equilibrium set of prices is that which brings demand and supply into equality in each market. In the absence of microeconomic imperfections within individual markets (for example, the existence of monopoly power or externalities) the outcome can be shown to be Pareto efficient.

Keynesian macroeconomics adopts the position that the price mechanism is not sufficiently effective to ensure that markets clear continuously. Instead, we may observe situations of disequilibrium which persist for significant periods of time. The effect of this is that the observed state of the economy[1] at any point in time is likely to be Pareto inefficient. Thus the Keynesian equilibrium is one in which market failure is a dominant feature and in which government policy to correct such failures is a real possibility.

Now there are two ways in which we can approach Keynesian economics. The first is to take the failure of markets as given and to analyse the implications for macroeconomic performance. This, in general, will be the approach taken throughout this chapter. The second, and equally important, side to Keynesian economics concerns the microeconomic foundations of the market failures which give rise to macroeconomic inefficiencies. This approach is often given the title 'New Keynesian' economics, particularly in the United States. We will return to this topic in Chapter 5 when we examine the labour market in greater detail.

4.1 Comparative statics of the Keynesian model

The first stage of our analysis is to examine the formalization of the Keynesian model by Hicks (1937). According to this approach, the two major theoretical innovations in the Keynesian General Theory are the consumption function, which can be shown to give rise to the multiplier process, and the liquidity preference theory of the demand for money. These in turn determine the equilibrium conditions in the markets for goods and money.

The structure of the Keynesian model is as follows:

$$C = C(Y) \qquad 0 < C_Y < 1 \tag{4.1}$$

$$I = I(r) \qquad I_r < 0 \tag{4.2}$$

$$Y \equiv C + I + G \tag{4.3}$$

$$M^d = L(Y, r) \qquad L_Y > 0, \quad L_r < 0 \tag{4.4}$$

$$M^s = \bar{M} \tag{4.5}$$

$$M^d = M^s \stackrel{.}{=} \bar{M} \tag{4.6}$$

Y is the level of national income or output, C is consumption, I is investment, r is the rate of interest, G is government spending and M is the money stock. Equation (4.1) is the Keynesian consumption function which relates aggregate consumption expenditures to real income. Equation (4.2) is the investment function which relates aggregate investment to the rate of interest. Equation (4.4) is a composite money demand function in which transactions and asset/speculative demands are combined, resulting in a function which depends on both income and the interest rate. Equation (4.5) states the assumption that the money supply is determined exogenously to the system. Equations (4.3) and (4.6) are equilibrium conditions for the goods and money markets, respectively. Although Eq. (4.3) is true by definition when dealing with *ex post*, or realized, expenditure flows, it is not true by definition for *ex ante*, or planned expenditures. Therefore in solving for the equilibrium of the system Eq. (4.3) is used as an equilibrium condition between planned expenditures rather than as an accounting identity. Since it will simplify notation to work with the savings function rather than the consumption function, we rewrite Eqs (4.1) and (4.3) as:

$$S = S(Y) \qquad 0 < S_Y < 1 \tag{4.1a}$$

$$S \equiv I + G \tag{4.3a}$$

We are now in a position to solve for the equilibrium of this system and to derive its comparative static properties. We begin by deriving the slopes of the equilibrium loci in r, Y space for the goods and money markets.

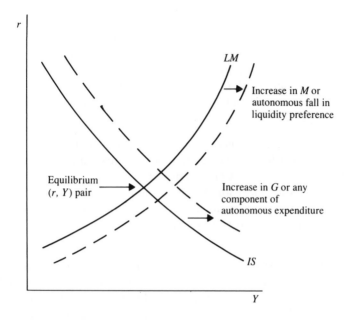

Figure 4.1 Equilibrium in the *IS–LM* model

In the case of the goods market the equilibrium condition is obtained by substituting Eqs (4.1a) and (4.2) into (4.3a). This yields the familiar *IS* relationship between income and the interest rate which defines goods market equilibrium. The slope of this relationship can be found by total differentiation to be:

$$\frac{\mathrm{d}r}{\mathrm{d}Y}\bigg|_{IS} = \frac{S_Y}{I_r} \tag{4.7}$$

Since S_Y is positive and I_r is negative, this means that the *IS* curve must be downward sloping.

Now consider equilibrium in the money market. Setting demand equal to the exogenous supply and totally differentiating we obtain:

$$\frac{\mathrm{d}r}{\mathrm{d}Y}\bigg|_{LM} = -\frac{L_Y}{L_r} \tag{4.8}$$

and since L_Y is positive and L_r is negative this function is upward sloping. Taken together, these are sufficient conditions for a unique equilibrium interest rate and income level to exist for given values of government spending and the money supply. The equilibrium is shown in Fig. 4.1, along with the effects on the two equilibrium loci of disturbances in the exogenous variables. The *IS* curve moves outwards in response to an increase in government spending or any other component of autonomous expenditure. The *LM* curve shifts outwards in response to an increase in the money stock or an autonomous fall in liquidity preference.

The Keynesian equilibrium differs from that of the Classical model in two important ways:

1. The real and financial sectors are linked through the rate of interest. Thus 'money matters' in the determination of real output whereas it was completely neutral in the Classical model.
2. There is no requirement for the equilibrium level of income to coincide with that corresponding to full employment. In other words, the outcome may be Pareto sub-optimal in that there are unrealized gains from trade.

Bearing these properties of the equilibrium in mind, we now turn to the comparative static effects of changes in government spending and the money supply. To derive the output multiplier with respect to government spending, take the total derivatives of the goods and money market equilibrium conditions, but this time allow for a change in G. This yields a pair of equations of the form:

$$S_Y \, dY - I_r \, dr = dG \tag{4.9a}$$

$$L_Y \, dY + L_r \, dr = 0 \tag{4.9b}$$

Using Eq. (4.9b) to eliminate dr from (4.9a) and dividing by dG yields the government expenditure multiplier:

$$\frac{dY}{dG} = \frac{1}{S_Y + I_r L_Y / L_r} \tag{4.10}$$

Providing all the partial derivatives have their expected signs then this is unambiguously positive. The advantage of deriving Eq. (4.10) in this very general form is that we have not as yet had to make any specific assumption about the values of the relevant elasticities and hence the shapes of the *IS* and *LM* curves.

The effect of G on the rate of interest can be derived by using Eq. (4.9b) to eliminate dY from Eq. (4.9a). The result is given by:

$$\frac{dr}{dG} = \frac{-1}{I_r + S_Y L_r / L_Y} \tag{4.11}$$

Under standard assumptions about the signs of the partial derivatives, this can be shown to be positive. Thus the net effect of an increase in government spending, keeping the money supply constant, is to increase output and interest rates. The size of the effect on both variables is determined by the size of the partial derivatives of the behavioural functions which make up the model.

Turning to monetary policy, we can derive the output multiplier with respect to changes in the stock of money in the same way as we derived the government expenditure multiplier. Total differentiation yields the following pair of equations:

$$S_Y \, dY - I_r \, dr = 0 \qquad (4.12a)$$

$$L_Y \, dY + L_r \, dr = dM \qquad (4.12b)$$

Using Eq. (4.12a) to eliminate dr from (4.12b) we obtain the following expression:

$$\frac{dY}{dM} = \frac{1}{L_Y + L_r S_Y / I_r} \qquad (4.13)$$

which is positive under the normal sign restrictions on the partial derivatives. We will use the term *monetary policy multiplier* to describe the expression given by Eq. (4.13). This is to distinguish it from the *money multiplier*, which relates the stock of money to the monetary base (cf. Chapter 7).

The effect of changes in the stock of money on the rate of interest can be derived as:

$$\frac{dr}{dM} = \frac{1}{L_r + L_Y I_r / S_Y} \qquad (4.14)$$

The expression given in Eq. (4.14) is negative under the usual sign restrictions.

Much of the debate between Keynesian and monetarist schools of thought during the 1960s and 1970s was concerned with the relative effectiveness of fiscal and monetary policy, i.e. the relative size of the government expenditure and monetary policy multipliers. While this is ultimately an empirical question, we can use the theoretical model we have developed to identify the circumstances under which one type of policy is more or less powerful than the other. To do this, we derive the effects on the policy multipliers of changes in the parameters of the underlying behavioural functions, as embodied in the partial derivatives of those functions. The results of this exercise are given in Table 4.1.

A number of special cases have figured prominently in the literature. These arise from extreme assumptions about the partial derivatives of the

Table 4.1 Effects of increase in derivatives of behavioural functions on absolute values of policy multipliers

	dY/dG	dr/dG	dY/dM	dr/dM
S_Y	−	−	−	+
I_r	−	−	+	−
L_Y	−	+	−	−
L_r	+	−	−	−

+ indicates an increase, − indicates a decrease

behavioural functions. While it is unlikely that these assumptions are satisfied in practice, it is nevertheless instructive to look at these cases.

Case 1: Interest-inelastic investment $I_r = 0$

If this is the case then $dY/dG = 1/S_Y$ and $dY/dM = 0$. This is the maximum possible value for the government expenditure multiplier and corresponds to the solution given by the Keynesian cross-diagram in which the monetary sector is ignored. The monetary policy multiplier is zero, since a fall in interest rates due to a monetary expansion has no stimulating effect on investment expenditures. Fiscal policy is said to have its full multiplier effect since there is no crowding out through the interest rate.

Case 2: The liquidity trap $L_r \to \infty$

Again, this implies that $dY/dG = 1/S_Y$ and $dY/dM = 0$. However, the reasons for these results are somewhat different. In this case, monetary policy is ineffective because the interest rate cannot be pushed any lower, not because the interest rate does not affect investment. The government expenditure multiplier is at its maximum since there is no indirect crowding out, due to the fact that the interest rate does not rise in response to a fiscal expansion.

Case 3: Interest-inelastic demand for money $L_r = 0$

This implies $dY/dG = 0$ and $dY/dM = 1/L_Y$. Here fiscal policy is rendered powerless because of powerful crowding-out effects. Monetary policy is at its most potent in this case.

How general is Hicks's *IS–LM* version of the General Theory? In some ways it marks a very distinct advance on the Classical macroeconomic model. The incorporation of the liquidity preference theory of the demand for money gives rise to a much richer set of interactions between the goods and money markets than was possible, given the restrictive assumption of a fixed velocity of circulation. However, in one important way the *IS–LM* model is considerably less general—it leaves the labour market out of the analysis, thus neglecting the supply side completely. The result of this is that employment responds passively to changes in output—the economy slides up and down the short-run production function according to the equilibrium determined by the intersection of the *IS* and *LM* curves. Although it is necessary to know the wage and price levels in order to calculate the *IS–LM* equilibrium the determination of these variables is not brought into the analysis in any meaningful way. In the next section we go on to discuss one route by which the labour market is brought into the model. This gives rise to the aggregate demand–aggregate supply (AD–AS) analysis which is now popular in many textbooks.

4.2 The supply side in the static Keynesian model

Modigliani (1944) added a supply side to the *IS–LM* model by building on Keynes's acceptance of the first classical postulate—that the real wage should equal the marginal product of labour. Together with the assumption that the money wage is fixed, or at least sticky, while the price level is perfectly flexible, this provides the basis of the supply side of the model.

The *IS–LM* system provides the basis for the demand side of the economy. It can be solved to obtain an expression relating the aggregate demand for goods to government spending and the money supply as in Eq. (4.15). Since we now intend to make the price level endogenous we naturally replace M by M/P, the level of the real money stock, and write this as:

$$Y^d = Y^d(M/P, G) \qquad Y^d_{M/P} > 0, \quad Y^d_G > 0 \tag{4.15}$$

or

$$Y^d = Y^d(M, P, G) \qquad Y^d_M > 0, \quad Y^d_P < 0, \quad Y^d_G > 0 \tag{4.15a}$$

The partial derivatives[2] Y^d_G and Y^d_M are, respectively, the government expenditure and monetary policy multipliers of the *IS–LM* model. The properties of the supply side of the economy can be shown to depend on the characteristics of the short-run production function. For the first Classical postulate to be satisfied the marginal product of labour must equal the real wage: alternatively, the money wage should equal the marginal revenue product of labour. This can be written:

$$\frac{dY}{dN} P = W \tag{4.16}$$

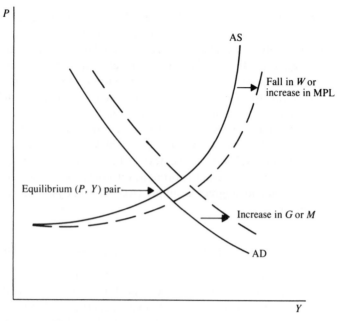

Figure 4.2 Equilibrium in the AD–AS model

or defining $\mu(Y)$ to be equal to the marginal product of labour, where μ is a downward-sloping function of the level of output, we can solve for the price level as:

$$P = \frac{W}{\mu(Y)} \qquad (4.16a)$$

where $\mu_Y < 0$. This defines the aggregate supply curve for output.

Since we now have expressions for both demand and supply side equilibrium we are in a position to solve for the comparative static properties of the system. Total differentiation of Eqs (4.15a) and (4.16a) yields a pair of equations of the form:

$$dY = Y_P^d \, dP + Y_M^d \, dM + Y_G^d \, dG \qquad (4.17a)$$

$$P\mu_Y \, dY + \mu(Y) \, dP = dW \qquad (4.17b)$$

Note that there are now three exogenous variables within the system—M, G and W. There are also three endogenous variables—Y, P and r (though the rate of interest does not appear explicitly since it was eliminated when the aggregate demand curve was constructed). We can calculate the effects of changes in the exogenous variables in the same way as we did for the *IS*–

Table 4.2 Comparative statics of the flexible price Keynesian model

	$\mathrm{d}Y$		$\mathrm{d}P$	
$\mathrm{d}G$	$\dfrac{\mu Y_G^{\mathrm{d}}}{\mu + PY_P^{\mathrm{d}}\mu_Y}$	> 0	$\dfrac{PY_G^{\mathrm{d}}\mu_Y}{\mu + PY_P^{\mathrm{d}}\mu_Y}$	> 0
$\mathrm{d}M$	$\dfrac{\mu Y_M^{\mathrm{d}}}{\mu + PY_P^{\mathrm{d}}\mu_Y}$	> 0	$\dfrac{PY_M^{\mathrm{d}}\mu_Y}{\mu + PY_P^{\mathrm{d}}\mu_Y}$	> 0
$\mathrm{d}W$	$\dfrac{Y_P}{\mu + PY_P^{\mathrm{d}}\mu_Y}$	< 0	$\dfrac{1}{\mu + PY_P^{\mathrm{d}}\mu_Y}$	> 0

LM system. However, in this case we must also consider the additional exogenous variable, *W*. The nature of the equilibrium can be shown in the Aggregate Demand–Aggregate Supply (AD–AS) diagram given in Fig. 4.2. The comparative static results are presented in Table 4.2.

μ_Y measures the way in which the marginal product of labour responds to changes in output. It is therefore capturing the flexibility of the production technology. If μ_Y is close to zero then extra workers can be taken on, and extra output produced, without a significant drop in productivity. Such a scenario would be plausible in a recession, when the pool of labour available for hiring contains a significant fraction of high-productivity workers. In contrast, during a boom we would expect there to be little unused capacity, and the pool of unemployed labour available to consist mainly of low-productivity workers. Thus during a boom we would expect μ_Y to be large in absolute value, as the marginal product of labour declines sharply with small increases in output.

If $\mu_Y = 0$ then both the government expenditure and the monetary policy multipliers are equal to the values which would be derived from *IS–LM* analysis. Also, if $\mu_Y = 0$ then changing *G* or *M* has no effect on the price level. Thus the fixed-price Hicksian *IS–LM* model is most appropriate in situations where the level of output is well below capacity and therefore the marginal product of labour is approximately constant. If μ_Y is allowed to become arbitrarily large then the reverse occurs, with the government expenditure and monetary policy multipliers becoming zero and prices adjusting fully in both cases. Thus the AD–AS model permits a resolution of Friedman's (1971) 'missing equation' problem. The division between the price and output response to an expansionary policy is determined by the responsiveness of the marginal product of labour to changes in output.

4.3 Keynesian approaches to the business cycle

In the form in which we have presented it, the Keynesian model provides a theory of the determination of the equilibrium level of output, but not one of the business cycle. Keynes himself indicated that his theory might provide the basis for such a theory:

> The trade cycle is best regarded, I think, as being occasioned by a cyclical change in the marginal efficiency of capital, though complicated and often aggravated by associated changes in the other significant short-period variables of the economic system. (*General Theory*, Chapter 22, page 313)

However, Keynes did not go on to develop a formal model of the cycle. Samuelson (1939) was the first to attempt such a theory by combining the multiplier and accelerator process. Since his theory embodies many of the principal points of interest in Keynesian cycle theory, we will develop our discussion around it.

Let us assume a very simple economy in which there is no government or foreign trade. The economy is fully characterized by the following system of three equations:

$$Y_t \equiv C_t + I_t \tag{4.18}$$

$$C_t + \alpha Y_{t-1} \tag{4.19}$$

$$I_t = \beta(C_t - C_{t-1}) + \varepsilon_t \qquad \varepsilon_t \sim N(0, \sigma_\varepsilon^2) \tag{4.20}$$

Equation (4.18) is the national income accounting identity, Eq. (4.19) is the consumption function, in which consumption is assumed proportional to last period's income, and Eq. (4.20) is the accelerator function for investment expenditure, in which it is assumed that investment takes place when there is a growth in demand for capital goods by the consumer goods sector. Note that we have added an extra term to Samuelson's investment function in the form of the stochastic error term, ε. This enables us to discuss stochastic elements in the cyclical process and goes some way towards incorporating Keynes's idea that fluctuations in the marginal efficiency of capital are the root cause of the cycle. All variables are expressed in terms of deviations from their equilibrium values. Note that in moving to a dynamic model we need to index each variable by time.

By substituting Eqs (4.19) and (4.20) into the accounting identity we obtain an equation in Y only. This is given in

$$Y_t = \alpha(1 + \beta)Y_{t-1} - \alpha\beta Y_{t-2} + \varepsilon_t \tag{4.21}$$

This is a second-order difference equation in output with a stochastic disturbance term. This type of equation illustrates Frisch's (1937)

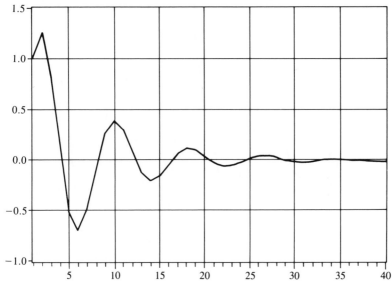

Figure 4.3 Response to unit disturbance. Alpha = 0.5, beta = 1.5

characterization of the cycle as a combination of a *propagation mechanism*, the deterministic part of the equation, and a source of *impulses*, the stochastic disturbance. Now in Samuelson's original paper there is no stochastic disturbance and therefore no exogenous source of impulses for the cycle. Nevertheless it is still possible for the deterministic part of Eq. (4.21) alone to exhibit cycles if the roots of the characteristic equation are complex. This is illustrated in Fig. 4.3 which shows the response of output to a once-and-for-all disturbance. However, except for certain freak values of the parameters, the cycles generated by a deterministic system will either die out eventually or increase in amplitude through time.

If we add a stochastic element to the model then the cycles generated appear to mimic real-world cycles much better. For example, Fig. 4.4 shows a simulated time path for output in which the propagation mechanism is the same as that in Fig. 4.3, but in which there is now a random disturbance term with mean zero and variance one. The cycles generated appear similar to those we observed for pre-1914 UK data (cf. Chapter 1, Figure 1.5) in that a fairly regular pattern emerges which does not damp down as time passes. Moreover, there is a surprising result from this type of stochastically disturbed equation in that, even if the propagation mechanism shows no inherent tendency for cycles to occur, the presence of a purely random stochastic disturbance will create an apparently cyclical pattern in the data. This is illustrated by Figs 4.5 and 4.6. In Fig. 4.5 we show the time path of

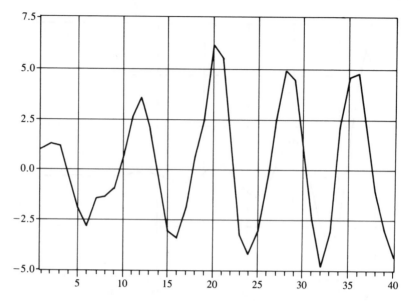

Figure 4.4 Stochastically disturbed equation. Alpha = 0.5, beta = 1.5

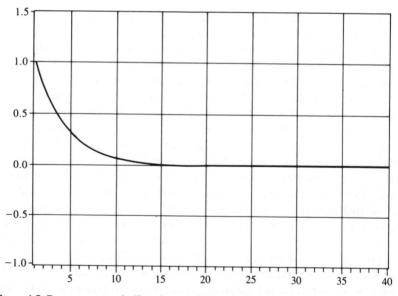

Figure 4.5 Response to unit disturbance. Alpha = 0.75, beta = 0.0

an economy subject to a once-and-for-all shock: it is evident that convergence to equilibrium is monotonic. In Fig. 4.6 we show the same

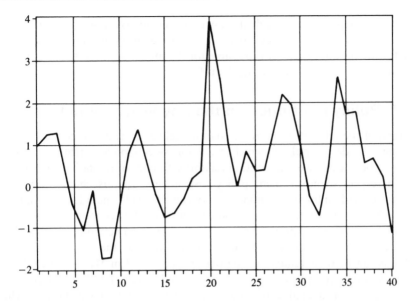

Figure 4.6 Stochastically disturbed equation. Alpha = 0.75, beta = 0.0

economy but now subjected to a stochastic disturbance in each period. Visual inspection of the series would indicate the existence of a regular cyclical pattern.

Our general conclusion is therefore that the combination of a lag structure in the behavioural relationships and the presence of stochastic disturbances is sufficient to produce the appearance of cycles in the data. This is not a new conclusion. In 1937 Slutsky showed that taking a ten-period moving average of random variables produced a series which behaved very similarly to an index of the British business cycle. This is essentially the same phenomenon that we have described here. The combination of a propagation mechanism (in Slutsky's case taking moving averages and in our case a second-order difference equation) and a random disturbance creates cycles in the data. Similar results were found by Adelman and Adelman (1959) and Adelman (1960) for simulations of the Klein–Goldberger macroeconomic model of the US economy. They showed that this model did not, in itself, produce cycles. That is, if the model is subjected to a single disturbance, convergence to equilibrium is monotonic. However, when the response of the model to a series of independent normally distributed disturbances is calculated, then it appears to mimic the business cycle very well.

To summarize: Keynesian theories of the cycle arise from combination of lags in the behavioural relationships, which give rise to the propagation mechanism, and stochastic disturbances, which act as the source of impulses or innovations to the model. Even if the propagation mechanism does not naturally produce cycles it is possible for the model to generate cycles if it is continually subject to stochastic disturbances.

4.4 Policy multipliers in the Keynesian model

Much of the interest in the Keynesian model stems from the possibilities of using it to design policies which will improve economic performance. For this to be feasible we must obtain reliable estimates of the policy multipliers with respect to government policy instruments. In this chapter we have concentrated on fiscal and monetary policies. We will conclude by examining the effectiveness of both types of policy within the UK economy.

In order to assess policy we must make use of an econometric model of the economy. A number of such models exist for the UK and a good discussion of their relative properties can be found in Wallis (ed.) (1989). The simulations given here were calculated using the Ready Reckoner package made available by Garry MacDonald and David Turner. This package simulates three of the larger macroeconomic models: those based at the National Institute for Economic and Social Research (NIESR), the London Business School (LBS) and the Treasury (HMT). While the Ready Reckoner simulations are reasonably accurate within the range of the historical variability of the series they are likely to break down with large policy changes.[3] Here we simulate fairly modest changes in the policy instruments within the NIESR model. Note that for both fiscal and monetary policy the simulations were carried out under the assumption of a fixed real exchange rate. This may be somewhat unrealistic in practice, but it enables us to isolate the purely domestic, or closed economy, channels of policy that are discussed in this chapter.

We will consider fiscal policy first. The experiment undertaken is, *ceteris paribus*, an increase in government current expenditure of £2 billion at 1989 prices. It is assumed that this increase is maintained in each subsequent year. Two billion pounds amounts to about 2 per cent of total government current expenditure in 1989. The impact on the key endogenous variables is given in Table 4.3.

From the first row of Table 4.3 we see that the effect on GDP takes place mainly within the first year of the policy. Similarly, the rows corresponding to employment and unemployment show the bulk of the effect of the fiscal expansion coming in the first year with relatively minor effects in years 2 and 3. Taking the ratio of the increase in GDP to the initial increase in government spending, we calculate a multiplier of about 1.27, rising to 1.32, which seems low by the standards of many introductory textbook exposi-

Table 4.3 Effects of a £2 billion increase in government current expenditure in the NIESR model

	After 1 year	After 2 years	After 3 years
GDP (£m 1989 prices)	2547	2583	2642
Multiplier	1.27	1.29	1.32
Employment (000s)	116	130	136
Unemployment	−42	−55	−64
Price inflation (% p.a.)	0.2	0.5	0.2
Increase in PSBR per job created (£ 1989 prices)	9482	7692	8088

Table 4.4 Effects of a 2 per cent cut in short-term interest rates in the NIESR model

	After 1 year	After 2 years	After 3 years
GDP (£m 1989 prices)	1528	3061	4100
Employment (000s)	20	64	110
Unemployment	−8	−30	−52
Price inflation (% p.a.)	0.1	0.3	0.5

tions but would appear reasonable in comparison with most studies on large-scale macroeconometric models. The model does indicate a lag in the response of price inflation to the expansion, with the main effect coming in year 2. Finally, the 'cost' of creating employment, as measured by the increase in the PSBR per job created, is between £7500 and £9500.

The response to a monetary expansion is somewhat different. In the UK, monetary policy has traditionally operated through variations in interest rates rather than direct control over the money stock. In order to simulate the effects of a monetary expanion, a 2 per cent cut in the short-term interest rate is therefore considered. Again this is well within normal historical variations of this variable, so the simulations should be reasonably close to those which would be obtained from the full NIESR model. Table 4.4 gives the results.

In contrast with the case of fiscal policy, the effects of a monetary expansion are spread over a number of years. Both output and employment take about three years to adjust fully. This is probably because monetary policy operates through the channel of stimulating investment expenditure via low interest rates. Since it takes time for investment plans to be changed and implemented, there will be a significant lag before the effects of the policy are felt. In the case of a fiscal expansion there is an immediate effect on aggregate demand of the increase in government spending, followed by the working out of the multiplier process. On the basis of these simulations, this would appear to be complete within one year compared with three years for monetary policy.

4.5   How Keynesian is the 'Keynesian' model?

This chapter has presented the Keynesian model as it was developed by the work of Hicks and Modigliani. A question often raised is, to what extent can these versions of Keynes's theory be said to capture the spirit of the analysis of the General Theory? Some economists, mainly those who label themselves Post-Keynesian, have argued strongly that it does not. Their grounds for so arguing are that, by reducing Keynes's vision to a mechanical model in the way presented here, important subtleties are missed and the role of expectations, emphasized strongly by Keynes, is pushed into the background. The *IS–LM* and AD–AS models are described, in a somewhat dismissive manner, as 'Hydraulic'[4] or 'Bastard' Keynesianism. A more neutral term is 'Neo-Keynesian', which distinguishes these models from the analysis of the General Theory, but without pejorative overtones.

What should we make of these criticisms of the Neo-Keynesian approach? On balance I would tend to agree with Blaug's (1985) assessment that 'On re-reading the General Theory, one is struck by how much of what Keynes says does indeed resemble the supposedly vulgar interpretation of the Hicks–Hansen *IS–LM* apparatus' (1985, page 670).

This is not to deny the theoretical importance of the General Theory. Keynes was the first economist to attempt seriously the task of assembling a coherent general equilibrium macroeconomic model which was capable of explaining the problems of his era. Hicks and Modigliani formalized the essence of his model and made it accessible to the mass of economists. In the process of doing so, whole sections of the General Theory were ignored, but it is arguable that this was to the benefit of the development of macroeconomics as a discipline. Keynes's wilder flights of poetic fancy may make entertaining reading, but they form a poor basis for a consistent model of the macroeconomy. However, it is certainly true that for many years the Hicks–Modligliani type models neglected the role of expectations in the determination of macroeconomic equilibrium. Keynes has some serious points to make about uncertainty and expectations which make interesting reading from the point of view of modern macroeconomics. It is only with the development of the rival paradigm of New Classical macroeconomics (cf. Chapter 3) that expectations returned to the centre of the debate.

The problems with the Keynesian models are not that they ignore the

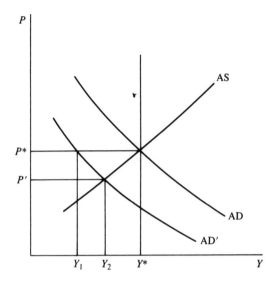

Figure U4.1.1 Stabilizing effects of price flexibility

hidden subtleties of Keynes's true message. Instead, the main problem is the lack of adequate microfoundations provided by Keynes. This, in itself, does not destroy the usefulness of the approach since it is a perfectly valid research strategy to take certain parameters as given in formulating a theory. However, economists have obviously sought to complete the Keynesian theory by providing it with a foundation in microeconomics. The New Keynesian economics involves the use of models of imperfect competition which naturally give rise to the rigidities of wages and/or prices which are the basis of the Neo-Keynesian models described in this chapter.

Unit 4.1

Does increasing price flexibility stabilize output?

Within the standard AD–AS model it is obvious that price flexibility will tend to stabilize fluctuations in output in response to changes in aggregate demand. This is illustrated in Fig. U4.1.1, which shows the response to fall in aggregate demand which shifts the AD curve from AD to AD'. If prices are fixed at P^* then output falls from the full employment level Y^* to Y_1. However, if the price level is free to fall then there will be a new short-run equilibrium of the economy in which the price level is P' and output has fallen to Y_2. What has happened is that the negative aggregate demand effects have, to some extent, been offset by a positive aggregate supply effect produced by a lower price level. It would

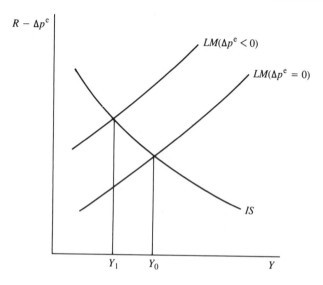

Figure U4.1.2 Destabilizing effects of price flexibility

therefore seem self-evident that increasing the degree of price flexibility in the economy will act to stabilize the fluctuations in output around its natural level.

However, one problem with the above argument is that it is purely static in nature. It compares one comparative static equilibrium with another but it does not provide any story about the dynamic adjustment process associated with the existence of unemployment and a falling price level. When we take into account these dynamic effects it is no longer obvious that price flexibility will be stabilizing for the economy.

Tobin (1975) provides a dynamic model which shows that price flexibility can have destabilizing as well as stabilizing effects. The crucial factor in his model is the effect of a falling price level on inflationary expectations. If price falls create the expectation of a continuing downward trend in the price level, then this will raise the real rate of interest for any given nominal rate, and this in turn will lower the level of aggregate demand. The destabilizing effects of this can be illustrated using the *IS–LM* diagram as shown in Fig. U4.1.2. On the vertical axis we have the real rate of interest, i.e. the nominal rate, R, minus the expected rate of inflation Δp^e. The *IS* curve shows a downward-sloping relationship between the real rate of interest and the real level of output. When we turn to the *LM* curve, however, we must remember that it is the *nominal* rate of interest which constitutes the opportunity cost of holding money. Hence the position of the *LM* curve in the figure will shift as the expected rate of inflation changes. In particular, a fall in expected inflation will move the *LM* curve from *LM* to *LM'* and create a new short-run equilibrium in which the real rate of interest is higher and real output is lower.

The above argument illustrates why, in the short run, a *falling* price level may reduce aggregate demand and lower output. Of course, it is still the case that the effects of a *lower* price level are to increase demand, so if the deflation continues for long enough, demand and output will begin to expand if this effect dominates. Tobin provides a complete dynamic model to explore the conditions under which the economy will converge on full employment equilibrium or under which it will be unstable. One problem with this model is, however, that it assumes that expectations of inflation are formed according to the adaptive expectations hypothesis (cf. Chapter 5 for a more detailed discussion). De Long and Summers (1986) have taken the same basic argument but have embedded it in a model with rational expectations and wage stickiness caused by the existence of overlapping contracts. They show, using numerical simulations, that it is possible for an increase in price flexibility to destabilize output even when inflationary expectations are rational.

Unit 4.2

Non-linear dynamics and deterministic chaos

Economists have, for the most part, confined themselves to dynamic models which can be represented as linear difference (or differential) equation systems. An example is the Samuelson multiplier accelerator model of the trade cycle presented in this chapter. However, such models have a drawback in that they do not generate endogenous fluctuations similar to those observed in the real world. In order to create business cycles of the type observed in economic time series we have to add stochastic disturbances to a linear difference equation specification.

Recent developments in the mathematical analysis of dynamic systems have shown that it is not necessary to include stochastic disturbances to models to generate apparently random-looking time series. This branch of mathematics has become known as *chaos theory*, since it shows that apparently simple, deterministic mathematical equations can produce exceedingly complex dynamic time paths.

Let us take as an example the logistic growth equation which is much used in biological sciences to describe the growth dynamics of populations:

$$\Delta y_t = g y_{t-1} (1 - y_{t-1}) \tag{U4.2.1}$$

where y_t is the size of the population relative to the carrying capacity of the environment at date t and g is the exogenous rate of growth of the population. This equation is non-linear, in that if the expression on the right-hand side is expanded, then we see that it includes the square of the endogenous variable as well as its first power. However, the equation does not include any random or stochastic elements—it is purely deterministic.

Now let us consider what kind of time path will be generated by an equation of this form. First, we need to find what, if any, equilibrium solutions exist. Expanding the equation and setting $y_t = y_{t-1} = \bar{y}$, we obtain a quadratic equation in y which has two solutions, $y = 0$ and $y = 1$. Suppose we begin with an initial value of the population which is not equal to either of these equilibrium values. For low values of g (less than 3.73) then the logistic growth equation generates a smooth convergence of y on one of the equilibria or a stable cycle around it.

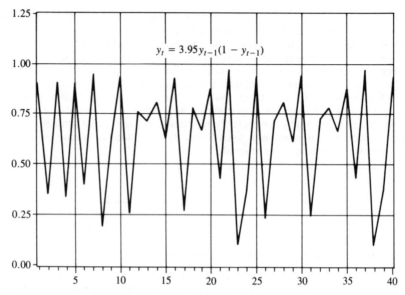

Figure U4.2.1 Time path generated by the logistic growth model

However, if the growth rate is above this critical value then convergence is anything but smooth. Instead, we have the appearance of random noise in the series, despite the fact that there is a purely deterministic mechanism at work. Figure U4.2.1 illustrates the type of chaotic time path we have been discussing. Starting from an initial value of $y = 0.9$ and with a value of $g = 4$, the progress of y through time gives all the appearances of having been generated by a random process.

Review questions

1. Consider the following simple economy:
   $Y = C + I + G$ National Income Accounting Identity
   $C = b(1 - t)Y$ Consumption Function
   where t is the exogenous tax rate.
   (a) Derive the multiplier for this economy.
   (b) Show that the existence of a government which imposes taxes that are proportional to income acts as an automatic stabilizer for the economy.
2. Consider the following simple economy:
   $Y_t = C_t + I_t + G_t$
   $C_t = b(1 - t)Y_t$
   $I_t = v(Y_t - Y_{t-1})$
   (a) Derive an expression for Y_t conditional on Y_{t-1}.

(b) Suppose $b = 0.8$, $t = 0.25$ and $v = 0.1$. If government spending equals 100, compute the equilibrium level of output.

(c) If Y_0 is equal to 150, compute the time path of output from time period 1 to time period 5. Plot your results on a graph.

3. Contrast the Keynesian model with the Neo-Classical model in terms of the linkages between the real and monetary sectors. What factors lead to the breakdown of the Classical Dichotomy in the Keynesian model?

4. Carefully trace out the effects on output and employment of an exogenous increase in labour productivity within the Keynesian model. In what ways do these differ from those which would be observed in the Neo-Classical model?

Federal Republic of Germany: GDP and investment

	GDP	*GFCF*
1961	4.6	6.7
1962	4.7	4.0
1963	2.8	1.4
1964	6.7	11.4
1965	5.5	4.7
1966	2.9	1.2
1967	−0.1	−6.9
1968	5.6	3.6
1969	7.5	9.8
1970	5.1	9.4
1971	2.9	6.1
1972	4.2	2.7
1973	4.7	−0.3
1974	0.3	−9.6
1975	−1.6	−5.3
1976	5.4	3.6
1977	3.0	3.6
1978	2.9	4.7
1979	4.2	7.2
1980	1.4	2.8
1981	0.2	−4.8
1982	−0.6	−5.3
1983	1.5	3.2
1984	2.8	0.8
1985	2.1	0.1
1986	2.6	3.1
1987	1.6	1.5
1988	2.1	6.4
1989	5.4	7.6
1990	3.5	5.2

Source: Eurostat

5. The data in the table on p. 79 show year-on-year percentage changes in real GDP and Gross Domestic Fixed Capital Formation for the Federal Republic of Germany. Plot both of them on a graph and use it to examine if the accelerator model works well.

Notes

1. Many authors reserve the term 'equilibrium' for states in which all gains from trade have been realized, i.e. Pareto-efficient outcomes. Thus the debate over whether a particular outcome constitutes an equilibrium or not is often determined by the author's use of the English language rather than any matter of economic substance. Nevertheless, the phrase 'observed state of the economy' is, to say the least, somewhat cumbersome and so I propose to use the term 'equilibrium' within a Keynesian context on the strict understanding that it does not imply Pareto efficiency.

2. Note that if we assume that aggregate demand is homogenous of degree one in money and prices, then the partial derivatives on money and prices are linked according to the equation:

$$Y_M^d = -\frac{M}{P} Y_P^d$$

3. MacDonald and Turner (1990) discuss the properties of their package relative to the original models as follows:

   In taking linear combinations of ready reckoners to estimate the effect of a policy package we rely on model properties being approximately linear. Experience suggests that such assumptions are likely to hold for magnitudes of policy change which are within historical experience, however for much larger changes this assumption is likely to be less reliable.

4. Hydraulic Keynesianism can be found in its most literal form in the Phillips–Newlyn model located at the University of Leeds. This consists of a series of tanks connected by pipes. The flows of water between tanks represents the flows of expenditure between different sectors of the economy. The tendency of the model to spring leaks in unexpected places is argued to add to its descriptive realism.

5.
Wages, prices and the New Keynesian macroeconomics

5.1 The importance of microfoundations

In Chapters 3 and 4 we considered two radically different short-run macroeconomic models. The Classical model derives from the standard microeconomic principles of perfect competition in all markets and instantaneous price adjustment to ensure that markets clear. In contrast, the Keynesian model of Chapter 4 was constructed on the assumption that some degree of nominal rigidity in wages and/or prices results in market failure. This in turn leads to the possibility that an active government demand management policy can lead to a Pareto improvement on the solution determined by the uncontrolled market. Keynesian models of this type have been rightly criticized as lacking adequate microfoundations, since the type of behaviour they describe appears to be inconsistent with the actions of rational utility-maximizing agents.

The purpose of this chapter is to analyse the determination of wages and prices and, by providing alternative microfoundations based on market imperfections, to show that these are consistent with macroeconomic Keynesian models of Chapter 4. This approach has been given the label *New Keynesian* economics, since it seeks to complement the traditional Keynesian preoccupation with the demand side of the economy by specifying an appropriate supply side.

In the first three sections of the chapter we look at theories of wage and price setting which lead to the kind of rigidities that underlie Keynesian models. Section 5.2 considers the efficiency wage model in which the dependence of labour productivity on wages means that wages fail to adjust to clear markets in response to a variety of economic disturbances. Section 5.3 gives a brief introduction to the literature on implicit contracts. This is a vast area, and it would not be useful to attempt to go too deeply into it. Instead, we concentrate on a simple example in which differences in attitudes to risk lead to firms offering workers insurance by maintaining the value of wages as the marginal product of labour fluctuates. Both the above approaches emphasize the rigidity of real rather than nominal wages. However, it is arguable that the existence of nominal rigidities lies at the heart of Keynesian analysis. Such nominal rigidities can be generated by the near-rational, or menu-cost, models described in Sec. 5.4. These models emphasize the large macroeconomic effects of a failure of firms to adjust prices, even though the benefits to the individual firm of so doing are small.

Sections 5.5 and 5.6 move away from the microeconomic analysis of pricing decisions to consider the implications of wage and price setting for macroeconomic dynamics. In Sec. 5.5 we examine the Phillips curve, so long the mainstay of the supply side of macro models. The emphasis here is on the implications of government economic policy in response to nominal inertia. Section 5.6 extends the analysis to consider staggered or 'Taylor' contracts in which wage and price dynamics are generated partially by forward-looking behaviour.

5.2 The efficiency wage model

The basic idea behind the efficiency wage model is that the productivity of labour depends on the wage received. To capture this, let us assume a firm facing a production function of the form:

$$Y = F(N^*, \bar{K}) \tag{5.1}$$

where N^* is the labour input measured in efficiency units, i.e.

$$N^* = e(w)N \qquad e'(w) > 0 \tag{5.2}$$

The labour input in efficiency units is therefore equal to the conventional measure of labour input, N, which will usually be measured in hours, multiplied by a function of the real wage rate $e(w)$. Thus as the real wage rate increases, the productivity of labour also rises as a direct result.

Why should we assume that the productivity of labour depends on the wage rate? The initial motivation of the literature on the efficiency wage came from development economics, in which the level of physical efficiency was argued to increase as nutritional standards improved because of higher wages. This would not seem plausible for developed economies but there remain a number of arguments in favour of a relationship of the form of Eq. (5.2). One is that higher wages help to reduce labour turnover, thus increasing the average level of human capital per worker, due to the acquisition of firm-specific skills. A second argument, put forward by Shapiro and Stiglitz (1984), is that when employers find it difficult to monitor labour effort, higher wages may act to reduce shirking by increasing the cost to a worker of losing his or her job in the event of a random check by the employer finding them not working.

Whatever the reason for the efficiency wage effect, let us consider its impact on the profit-maximizing decisions of the firm concerning wages and employment. The firm is assumed to have profit function of the form:

$$\Pi = aF(N^*, \bar{K}) - wN \tag{5.3}$$

where a is a productivity shift parameter or a source of exogenous changes in the production function. The firm maximizes Eq. (5.3) subject to the efficiency wage equation (5.2) plus the condition that $w \geq \bar{w}$, where $\bar{w}$ is a lower bound on the wage rate that the firm can pay. The lower bound is determined by the wage rate available outside the firm. Assuming that this second condition is satisfied, we can solve for the profit-maximizing wage and employment levels by setting the first-order partial derivatives of Eq. (5.3) with respect to L and w equal to zero:

$$\partial\Pi/\partial N = aF'(N^*, \bar{K})e(w) - w = 0 \tag{5.4}$$

$$\partial\Pi/\partial w = aF(N^*, \bar{K})e'(w)N - N = 0 \tag{5.5}$$

These can easily be shown to yield a solution for the optimal wage rate of the form:

$$e'(w)w/e(w) = 1 \tag{5.6}$$

i.e. the elasticity of effort with respect to the wage rate should be equal to one. Note that the optimal wage rate does not depend on either the level of employment or on the productivity shift parameter, a. Thus real wages remain constant in the face of disturbances, which alter the position of the production function and therefore the level of employment.

A diagrammatic illustration may help to clarify the above point. Figure 5.1 shows the firm's equilibrium. The horizontal line w^* is the wage rate which satisfies Eq. (5.6). The downward-sloping line marked MPL_1 is the marginal product of labour curve as given by $aF'(N^*, \bar{K})e(w)$. Providing w^* is greater than the competitive wage rate $\bar{w}$, there will be involuntary unemployment equal to the distance $N_F - N_1$. Now consider the effect of a negative productivity shock which is captured in this model by a fall in a. The new marginal product of labour curve is given by MPL_2 and the new equilibrium level of employment is determined by its intersection with the w^* line. Involuntary unemployment increases to $N_F - N_2$.

Note the contrast between this model and the conventional labour market model of Chapter 3. In conventional Neo-Classical models

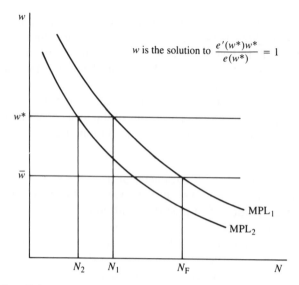

Figure 5.1 The efficiency wage model

involuntary unemployment is ruled out by the assumption that the real wage adjusts to clear the market. Moreover, the reaction to a productivity shock in Neo-Classical models is quite different. A fall in productivity would produce a fall in real wages and employment which would bring about a new market equilibrium. Thus the efficiency wage model provides results which are much closer to Keynesian models in that all the adjustment in response to a disturbance is borne by the volume of employment rather than by the price of labour.

5.3 Implicit contracts and wage stickiness

The implicit contracts theory of wage stickiness centres on the idea that workers are more risk-averse than firms. Because of this, firms offer workers insurance by agreeing to contracts which lead to wage fluctuations that are less than the underlying fluctuations in labour productivity. In the extreme case when firms are risk-neutral then wages do not vary with productivity at all. A thorough and accessible review of this literature can be found in Manning (1990).

To illustrate the implicit contracts theory, let us consider a very simple model. Workers and firms bargain over the wage rate that will be paid before they know what the level of labour productivity will be while the contract is in force. There are only two possible values that labour productivity can take with associated probabilities α and $(1 - \alpha)$. The level of employment is fixed. Given these assumptions, we can write the expected level of the workers' utility as:

$$E(u) = \alpha u(w_H) + (1 - \alpha)\, u(w_L) \qquad (5.7)$$

where w_H is the wage rate paid when the marginal product of labour is high and w_L is that paid when it is low. The utility function is assumed to embody some degree of risk-aversion, i.e. $u'(w) > 0$, $u''(w) < 0$. Thus workers are willing to trade off a reduction in the expected wage rate against a reduction in the dispersion of wage rates across the two possible states of the world that can occur.

Now consider the behaviour of the firm. In this case, we assume risk-neutrality. The reason for doing so is that the owners of the firm can spread their risks by holding shares in a number of different firms while workers must commit all their labour to the one firm. The firm wishes to minimize the expected cost of hiring labour, which is given by

$$E(c) = \alpha w_H + (1 - \alpha)w_L \qquad (5.8)$$

An efficient bargain will be one in which the marginal rate of substitution between w_H and w_L is the same for both parties. This can easily be shown to be satisfied when the conditions given by the following equation holds:

$$\frac{-(1 - \alpha)u'(w_L)}{\alpha u'(w_H)} = \frac{-(1 - \alpha)}{\alpha} \qquad (5.9)$$

The left-hand side of the above equation is the workers' marginal rate of substitution while the right-hand side is that of the firm. It is obvious that this equation can only be satisfied when the wage rate is the same under both states of nature, since we require $u'(w_L) = u'(w_H)$. Thus an efficient bargain is one in which the firm insures workers completely against fluctuations in wages due to exogenous changes in productivity. Again we can see parallels with the Keynesian idea that wages do not adjust to clear markets in response to disturbances.

A diagrammatic exposition of the above results may increase intuition. Figure 5.2 shows the determination of an efficient bargain. Workers have convex indifference curves and seek to maximize the distance from the origin. Firms have straight-line iso-cost curves and seek to get as close to the origin as possible. A bargain is efficient when one of the workers' indifference curves is tangential to one of the firm's iso-cost lines. From Eq. (5.9) this can only occur on the 45° line. Moreover, we are restricted to points on the 45° line above the point $(\bar{w}, \bar{w})$ (where $\bar{w}$ is the competitive wage rate available to workers outside the firm). Note that there is no reason to

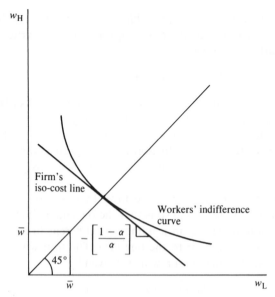

Figure 5.2 The implicit contracts model

expect there to be a unique efficient bargain. There may well be a range of tangencies on the 45° line corresponding to alternative efficient bargains. In order to choose between them, it would be necessary to bring in some idea of relative bargaining power between workers and firms.

5.4 Near-rational and menu-cost models

The models presented in Secs 5.2 and 5.3 give rise to stickiness in the *real* wage rate. While this leads to important insights for macroeconomic adjustment, it is arguable that it does not capture the important Keynesian idea that it is *nominal* stickiness which is responsible for many important business fluctuations. In particular, since the efficiency wage and implicit contract models determine real wage rates, then a monetary disturbance will leave their equilibria unchanged. Since a great deal of macroeconomics from Keynes onwards has been concerned with the effect of monetary conditions on real outcomes, this is unsatisfactory.

Two types of model have recently been put forward to·explain the apparent nominal stickiness observed in real-world economies. Near-rational models, pioneered by Akerlof and Yellen (1985), proceed on the assumption that firms do not change prices in response to nominal disturbances when the benefits of doing so are very small. Thus firms are nearly, but not fully, rational. A related approach developed by Mankiw

(1985) has adopted the idea of menu costs, i.e. whenever a firm changes a nominal price it incurs a small fixed cost associated with printing new menus, adjusting catalogue prices or any of a range of other alternatives. The near-rational and menu-cost approaches can be argued to be conceptually very close. In this section we develop a model based on that of Mankiw to illustrate how real equilibria are affected by nominal disturbances.

Consider an imperfectly competitive firm facing a downward-sloping inverse demand curve of the form:

$$P_i = f(q_i)M \tag{5.10}$$

where P_i and q_i are price and quantity for firm i and M is the value of the money stock for the whole economy. Firm i has a cost function in which total cost is proportional to output, with the nominal value of costs being determined by the money stock, i.e.

$$C_i = kqM \tag{5.11}$$

The money stock therefore acts as a scale variable for prices in this economy in exactly the same way as it does in the simple quantity theory version of the Neo-Classical macroeconomic model of Chapter 3. If we deflate both price and cost by the money stock then we can write the firm's condition for profit maximization as:

$$p + q\frac{dp}{dq} = \frac{dc}{dq} = k \tag{5.12}$$

where $p = P/M$ and $c = C/M$.

This is just the conventional condition that marginal revenue should equal marginal cost. For a linear demand curve the equilibrium can be shown as in Fig. 5.3. The equilibrium price and quantity are p_m and q_m, respectively, corresponding to the deflated price p_m, is a nominal price which can be written $P_m = p_m M$. The areas marked on the figure show the values taken by consumer surplus, producer surplus and monopoly welfare loss.

Suppose we now consider the impact of a cut in the money supply on the equilibrium of the firm. If the nominal price P_m remains fixed then there is a new equilibrium, p_0, q_0, in which output has fallen as shown in Fig. 5.4. However, the interesting question here is, under what circumstances will it prove optimal for the firm to keep its nominal priced fixed? By doing so it loses producer surplus to the value of the area $B - A$. The total welfare loss associated with a failure to adjust price is given by the sum of the loss of producer surplus and consumer surplus, $B + C$. Note that area A does not affect total welfare loss since it constitutes a transfer of consumer surplus to the producer.

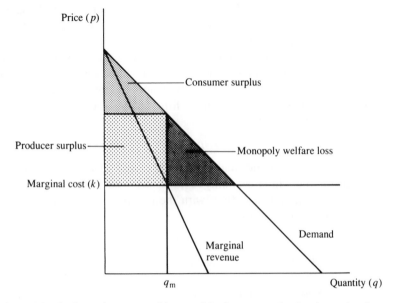

Figure 5.3 The imperfect competition model of output and price determination

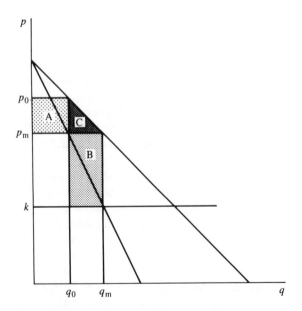

Figure 5.4 Effects of a cut in the money supply in the imperfect competition model with menu costs

We now reintroduce the idea of menu costs. Suppose the firm must incur a fixed cost, z, to change price. Providing $z > B - A$ then it is optimal for the firm to keep price constant. If $z > B + C$ then it is also socially optimal to keep price constant, but if $B + C > z > B - A$ then prices remain fixed, even though a general improvement in social welfare could be achieved by cutting them. This happens because the firm cannot appropriate all the benefits of the price cut. Part of it inevitably accrues as an increase in consumer surplus and so is disregarded in the firm's calculations.

The Mankiw model therefore illustrates, in a partial equilibrium context, why the degree of price flexibility may be less than is socially optimal. Note also that in this model it is possible for a *small* monetary expansion to raise output and increase social welfare at the same time. This would occur if the menu costs of increasing price were greater than the gain to the firm from so doing. The rise in social welfare comes about because of a reduction in monopoly welfare loss, but it will also involve a transfer of surplus away from the producer to consumers. The extent to which this can be done, however, is strictly limited. Once the monetary expansion becomes large enough such that the benefit to the firm of increasing price exceeds the menu cost, then prices will rise in proportion, and money once again becomes neutral with respect to real quantities.

5.5 Wage and price dynamics in a model with a Phillips curve

In Secs 5.1–5.3 we have considered the microeconomic foundations of wage- and price-setting behaviour which give rise to the kind of real and nominal rigidities that lead to Keynesian results. We now return to a more macroeconomic approach, in order to look at the implications of the existence of some form of inertia in wages and prices, for the dynamic behaviour of output and employment. Our starting point is the simple Phillips curve with adaptive expectations. This can be written:

$$p_t = p_{t-1} + \gamma y_t + \varepsilon_t \tag{5.13}$$

All variables are in natural logarithms. p_t can be interpreted as either the price level or its first difference, y_t is the ratio of real output to its natural level and ε_t is a stochastic error term or source of disturbance to prices. Suppose that real output depends on the level of real money balances according to

$$y_t = \phi(m_t - p_t) + v_t \tag{5.14}$$

where m_t is the logarithm of the nominal money stock and v_t is a stochastic demand disturbance. The model is closed by assuming a government policy rule of the form:

$$m_t = \beta p_t \tag{5.15}$$

where β measures the extent to which the policy authorities are willing to accommodate rises in the prices by increasing the money supply. Note that this model exhibits the natural rate property in that the long-run solution must be one in which $y_t = 0$, otherwise prices will continue to change.

By combining the three equations together, we obtain a first-order difference equation in prices of the form:

$$p_t = \alpha p_{t-1} + \alpha \gamma v_t + \alpha \varepsilon_t \tag{5.16}$$

where $\alpha = [1 - \gamma\phi\beta + \gamma\phi]^{-1}$. Because money and output depend on prices, Eq. (5.16) can also be used to derive equations for the time path of these variables, although we do not do so explicitly here. The coefficient α measures the degree of persistence of nominal shocks within the economy. A high value of α means a slow adjustment of prices and output to any kind of disturbance. Since the value of α depends on the policy rule adopted by the goverment, in that an increase in the value taken by β implies an increase in α, then the government retains the power to affect the time path the economy takes towards its long-run equilibrium, even though that equilibrium is outside its control. In the limit, if $\beta = 1$ then prices follow a random walk.

The importance of the choice of β is illustrated by the simulated response of the model to a unit disturbance to the price level. The coefficients γ and ϕ were set equal to 0.5 and 1.0, respectively, and the time paths of y and p were calculated for $\beta = 0.1$ (a 'non-accommodating' monetary rule) and $\beta = 0.9$ (an 'accommodating' monetary rule). Table 5.1 gives the values obtained by numerical simulation of the model and Fig. 5.5 illustrates the time paths of prices and output given in Table 5.1.

Under an accommodating monetary rule the price level takes a long time to adjust back towards its equilibrium level but output remains close to the natural rate throughout. With a non-accommodating rule the price level declines quickly after the initial shock but there are also severe short-term consequences for the output level. However, after seven time periods, the price decline has been sufficient to bring output closer to the natural rate than it is under the policy of accommodation.

That government policy matters in this model is a product of the fact that expectations of prices are backward-looking. This is implied by the specification of the Phillips curve equation (5.13), in which price expectations are set equal to the value observed in the previous period. By replacing the assumption of backward-looking, or adaptive, expectations with that of forward-looking or rational expectations, the dependence of the time path of output on government monetary policy would be eliminated. Thus the

Table 5.1 Accommodating and non-accommodating monetary rules in the Phillips curve model

T	Accommodating rule $\beta = 0.9$ $\alpha = 0.95$			Non-accommodating rule $\beta = 0.1$ $\alpha = 0.69$		
	p_t	y_t	m_t	p_t	y_t	m_t
1	0.95	−0.10	0.86	0.69	−0.62	0.07
2	0.91	−0.09	0.82	0.48	−0.43	0.05
3	0.86	−0.09	0.78	0.33	−0.30	0.03
4	0.82	−0.08	0.74	0.23	−0.20	0.02
5	0.78	−0.08	0.71	0.16	−0.14	0.02
6	0.75	−0.07	0.67	0.11	−0.10	0.01
7	0.71	−0.07	0.64	0.07	−0.07	0.01
8	0.68	−0.07	0.61	0.05	−0.05	0.01
9	0.64	−0.06	0.58	0.04	−0.03	0.00
10	0.61	−0.06	0.55	0.02	−0.02	0.00

results of the New Classical model of Chapter 3 would hold good.

5.6 Wage and price dynamics with staggered contracts

The backward-looking nature of the Phillips curve model in Sec. 5.4 is unsatisfactory in that it is inconsistent with the rational expectations hypothesis. At the same time, the Lucas model with rational expectations and an auction market for labour seems to ignore many of the important institutional characteristics of the labour market, and to fail to account for the sort of dynamic paths of wages, prices and output we observe in real-world economies. Taylor (1979, 1980) has set out a general model which includes pure backward-looking and pure forward-looking models as special cases.

Taylor's model is built around the idea of wage contracts which are set at different dates and which overlap with each other. The simplest possible case is if there is an annual wage round in which some contracts are agreed in January and others in June. Thus a bargainer setting the wage rate in January knows that, during the year in which the contract is in force, it will overlap with contracts set the previous June and also those set the following June. If bargainers care about relative wages then it therefore becomes necessary to look backward to those contracts already in force and forward to those which will be set during the coming year. This is formalized in the following wage equation:

$$x_t = bx_{t-1} + dx_{t+1}^e + \gamma(by_t^e + dy_{t+1}^e) + \varepsilon_t \qquad (5.17)$$

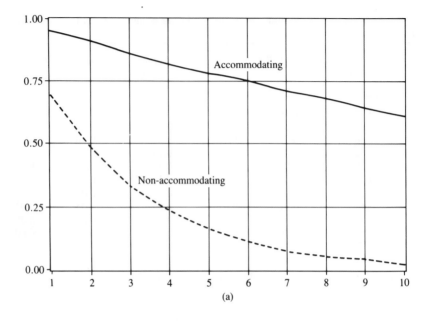

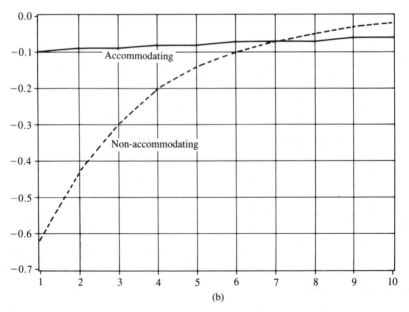

Figure 5.5 Time paths of (a) prices and (b) output under alternative monetary rules

where x_t is the contract wage set at date t. Contracts negotiated at date t depend on those negotiated in the previous period, the expectation of the contract wage in the next period, the expected value of excess demand in the current and following periods and a disturbance term ε. The coefficients b and d are the weights put on backward- and forward-looking behaviour and should sum to one. If $b = 1$ then the model reverts to one of pure backward-looking behaviour.

To make this model comparable with the standard Phillips curve we assume that prices are a constant mark-up on wages, so we can replace the contract wage with the price level. The price level observed will be an average of the contracts in force in any time period, i.e.

$$p_t = 0.5(x_t + x_{t-1}) \tag{5.18}$$

The model is then completed by adding the aggregate demand equation (5.14) and the monetary rule (5.15) specified for the Phillips curve. Solving this set of equations leads to the following equation describing the time path of the price level (see Appendix to this chapter):

$$p_t = \alpha p_{t-1} + 0.5(\varepsilon_t + \varepsilon_{t-1}) \tag{5.19}$$

Table 5.2 presents the simulated time path of an economy described by the above set of equations on the assumption that government adopts an accommodating monetary policy rule by setting $\beta = 0.9$ and that the forward- and backward-looking elements in the contract equation are given equal weight, i.e. $b = d = 0.5$ in Eq. (5.17). As in Table 5.1, it is assumed that the economy is shocked by a unit disturbance to price, i.e. $\varepsilon_1 = 1$ and 0 thereafter.

It is interesting to compare this simulation with that for the pure backward-looking Phillips curve in Table 5.1. In the earlier case the shock was assumed to affect the price level directly, thus raising price by a factor of 0.95 in the first period, once the dampening effect of the associated fall in output had been taken into account. Here the shock affects new contracts but not those already in existence, so the price level rises by only 0.5 in the first period. However, as contracts come up for renegotiation the price level is pushed up further, rising to 0.86 in the second period. After this, the disinflationary effect of falling real balances begins to dominate and the price level begins to fall. Because of the forward-looking nature of contracts, the fall is faster than in the case of the simple Phillips curve. This can be seen in Fig. 5.6, which compares the time paths of the price level under backward-looking expectations and Taylor contracts.

The fact that price adjusts faster in the initial period with the Phillips curve model may seem surprising given that agents are forward-looking in the Taylor contracts model. However, the reason for this is that we are

Table 5.2 Adjustment dynamics in an economy with Taylor contracts

Accommodating rule $\beta = 0.9$
$\alpha = 0.72$

T	p_t	y_t	m_t
1	0.50	−0.05	0.45
2	0.86	−0.09	0.78
3	0.63	−0.06	0.56
4	0.46	−0.05	0.41
5	0.33	−0.03	0.30
6	0.24	−0.02	0.22
7	0.18	−0.02	0.16
8	0.13	−0.01	0.11
9	0.09	−0.01	0.08
10	0.07	−0.01	0.06

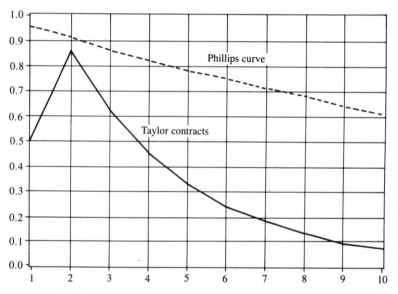

Figure 5.6 Response to price shock in Taylor contracts and Phillips curve models

implicitly making the assumption that wages and prices are set in auction markets in the Phillips curve model. There are no contracts to induce rigidity in either variable, and the only factor that prevents instantaneous adjustment is the sluggish reaction of expectations to disturbances.

5.7 Summary

The determination of wages and prices is at the centre of macroeconomic modelling. It is the failure of the Keynesian model to give an adequate microeconomic foundation for wage and price stickiness which is the major unsatisfactory feature of this type of model. At the same time, the New Classical procedure of treating wages as if they were set in auction markets leads to models which generate implausible predictions.

New Keynesian macroeconomics has made significant progress in recent years in redressing the shortcomings of the older Keynesian tradition. Models of the supply side have been put forward which generate the types of rigidity observed in real-world economies, and which create business cycles with Keynesian features. In this chapter we have considered the efficiency wage and implicit contract approaches to explaining the rigidity of real wages and the menu-cost approach to explaining the rigidity of nominal prices in response to monetary innovations. We have also discussed the importance of the existence of contracts in explaining the inertia of the wage and price level, and the consequent sluggish adjustment of output, even in the presence of rational expectations.

Unit 5.1

Hysteresis and the natural rate of unemployment

One of the problems facing proponents of the natural rate theory of unemployment is that unemployment rates do not, at first sight, appear to behave in a way that is consistent with this theory. If a natural rate exists then increases in unemployment should be temporary affairs, which disappear once inflationary expectations have had time to adjust and to become consistent with actual levels of inflation. In most European countries at least, this does not seem to be the case. Increases in unemployment are very rarely reversed within any sort of reasonable time span. Instead, there appears to be a pattern of events in which a rise in the unemployment rate produces a ratchet-like effect, as if the natural rate itself had risen.

During the 1980s a number of economists, dissatisfied with the simple natural rate theory, began to develop models in which the natural rate depended not only on labour market fundamentals but also on the history of the level of unemployment itself. These are grouped under the general heading of *hysteresis* models.

The most prominent of these models is one put forward by Blanchard and Summers in 1986. Their starting point is the contrast between the European and US experiences of unemployment illustrated by Fig. U5.1.1. In both regions there is a pronounced upward trend in the unemployment rate, but it is the behaviour of unemployment around this trend which is of most interest. While the United States experiences a number of periods of sharply rising unemploy-

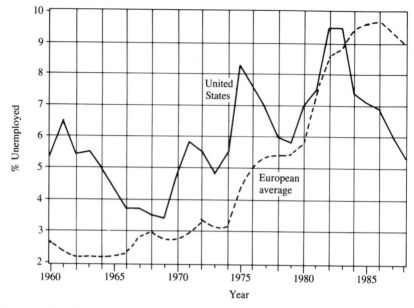

Figure U5.1.1 Average US and European rates of unemployment (per cent). (*Source:* Eurostat)

ment, these are usually quickly followed by periods in which unemployment falls back towards its trend growth path. The European series behaves quite differently in that periods of rising unemployment are followed, in the main, by periods in which the unemployment rate flattens out onto a plateau. This is the type of ratchet effect we have already mentioned.

What is it that permits unemployment in the United States to fall after a recession but appears to leave an entrenched increase in the natural rate in Europe? Blanchard and Summers argue that it is something fundamental about the comparative structure of labour markets between the two regions. Relative to the United States, European wage-bargaining structures are dominated by trades unions. These unions are normally concerned with maximizing the welfare of their members, and since workers' union membership normally lapses when they become unemployed, they effectively become outsiders in the wage-negotiation procedure. Hence, workers who have been unemployed long enough for their union membership to lapse no longer exercise any downward pressure on the rate of wage increase. In other words, the natural level of unemployment rises. This model of the wage-bargaining process has been given some empirical support for the UK by the work of Layard and Nickell (1986), who find that it is only short-term unemployment which acts to curb wage increases.

One implication of the idea of hysteresis is that it is no longer the case that the natural rate is determined solely by the supply side of the economy. A demand-led recession can produce a permanently higher level of unemployment if it is deep enough and if it persists for long enough. Thus in some ways the hysteresis argument is supportive of Keynesian ideas about the behaviour of the macroeconomy. However, this does not mean that naive Keynesian expansion policies will be enough to bring down both the actual, and the natural, rates of unemployment. An expansion may simply lead to higher wage inflation unless it is accompanied by policies to reduce the level of long-term unemployment and hence the natural rate.

Unit 5.2

Rational expectations and the Phillips curve

Since Milton Friedman's (1968) attack on the theoretical foundations of the Phillips curve it has been recognized that a proper treatment of expectations is essential if a good empirical specification is to be found. In many cases researchers have attempted to allow for the effect of price expectations by estimating equations of the form:

$$\Delta w_t = \alpha_0 - \alpha_1 u_t + \alpha_2 \Delta p_t^e + \varepsilon_t \qquad \text{(U5.2.1)}$$

where Δw_t is the rate of wage inflation, u_t is the percentage unemployed, Δp_t^e is a measure of expected inflation based on past observations of the inflation rate and ε_t is a random error term. They have then gone on to test the natural-rate hypothesis by testing if the coefficient on expected inflation equals one.

It has often come as a surprise to researchers in this area to find that the natural-rate hypothesis appears to be rejected by the data, in that the hypothesis that coefficient on expected inflation equals one also appears to be rejected by the data. However, in a recent paper by Alogoskoufis and Smith (1991) an argument has been put forward to suggest that this is only to be expected. The problem centres around the specification of the expected inflation term and, in particular, the use of a simple adaptive expectations mechanism. When a more satisfactory rational expectations framework is applied then the reasons for the apparent failure of the model become obvious.

To begin with, let us assume that inflation is generated by a first-order autoregressive process, i.e.:

$$\Delta p_t = \delta + \rho \Delta p_{t-1} + v_t \qquad \text{(U5.2.2)}$$

where v_t is a random, white-noise error, i.e. v is uncorrelated with its own past values and both the current and past values of Δp.

If this is the case then the rational expectation of inflation at date t is given by ρ multiplied by the actual inflation rate in the previous period. Now let us substitute this expectation into the Phillips curve Eq. (U5.2.1) to obtain:

$$\Delta w_t = \alpha_0(1 + \alpha_2 \delta) - \alpha_1 u_t + \alpha_2 \rho \Delta p_{t-1} + \varepsilon_t + \alpha_2 v_t \qquad \text{(U5.2.3)}$$

This equation looks superficially similar to the standard adaptive expectations augmented Phillips curve, in that it relates wage inflation to a constant, unemployment, lagged price inflation and a random error term. However, in this case we can see that the coefficient on lagged price inflation is not necessarily equal to one. Instead, it depends crucially on the degree of persistence in actual price inflation, as measured by the autoregressive parameter (ρ) in the process of generating price inflation. If ρ is close to zero then this implies that the last period's inflation rate is of little use in forecasting this period's rate, and so we would expect to find a low coefficient on lagged price inflation in an estimated Phillips curve.

The Phillips curve derived above also illustrates another problem associated with empirical work when agents are forming rational expectations. Since the coefficient on lagged price inflation in Eq. (U5.2.3) depends on the coefficient ρ, it will change if that coefficient changes. So, for example, if the government decides to accommodate inflation by relaxing its monetary policy, this will increase the persistence of inflation as measured by ρ. This in turn will show up as instability in the coefficient on lagged inflation in the estimated Phillips curve. Instability of this type is an example of what has become known as the *Lucas critique*, following the classic paper by Robert Lucas (1976), in which he argued that the coefficients of econometric models will tend to change if government policy rules change.

Alogoskoufis and Smith test for the presence of the kind of instability we have discussed above by estimating Phillips curve equations for the UK and the United States. They take a very long annual data set from 1857 to 1987 and examine two important sub-periods. These are the periods 1857–1913, in which monetary policy was strictly constrained by the operation of the international Gold Standard, and 1914–87, in which monetary policy tended to be much more accommodating. For the UK they find a value of ρ equal to 0.26 for the first period and 0.74 for the second, confirming the greater degree of inflation persistence. This is matched by a similar increase in the coefficient on lagged price inflation in the Phillips curve, from 0.30 in 1857–1913 to 0.91 in 1914–87. Thus the data appear to show exactly the sort of instability in the estimated coefficients which is predicted by the Lucas critique.

Review questions

1. Consider an economy which has a Phillips curve of the form:

$$p_t = p_{t-1} + 0.5y_t$$

   and an aggregate demand function of the form:

$$y_t = 1.5(m_t - p_t)$$

   (a) Derive an expression for the time path of the price level when the money stock is fixed at 1.
   (b) In what way does the Phillips curve need to be modified to take account of a growing money stock?

2. Consider an economy with an aggregate demand curve of the form:

$$y_t = 0.5(m_t - p_t)$$

   If the government adopts an accommodating monetary policy of the form:

$$m_t = 0.5p_{t-1} + 0.5p_{t-2}$$

   and there is a constant natural level of output, what will be the rational expectations time path for the price level?

3. Discuss the efficiency wage model, illustrating why:
   (a) It produces equilibrium unemployment.
   (b) Exogenous changes in labour productivity do not change employment.

4. Illustrate, using appropriate diagrams, why the existence of small costs for changing prices can produce large welfare effects.

5. The data in the table on p. 100 show wage inflation, unemployment and price inflation for the Italian economy. Use them to examine if the Phillips curve model fits well by calculating the rate of growth of the real wage and plotting this against the level of unemployment to see if the two are negatively correlated. If you have a regression package try estimating an equation of the form:

$$\Delta w_t = \beta_0 + \beta_1 U_t + \beta_2 \Delta p_{t-1}$$

   to see how well this fits.

Italy: Wage inflation, unemployment and price inflation

	Earnings	Unemployment	Price
1961	8.2	6.6	3.1
1962	13.5	5.5	6.0
1963	19.7	5.1	8.5
1964	12.3	5.2	6.3
1965	7.7	5.4	3.9
1966	7.9	5.9	2.4
1967	8.4	5.4	2.8
1968	7.4	5.7	1.8
1969	7.6	5.7	4.0
1970	15.7	5.5	7.2
1971	13.1	5.5	7.1
1972	11.1	6.4	6.3
1973	19.6	6.4	11.5
1974	22.1	5.4	18.4
1975	21.0	5.9	17.6
1976	20.9	6.8	17.9
1977	21.4	7.2	19.2
1978	16.2	7.3	13.9
1979	17.9	7.8	15.9
1980	22.5	7.7	20.6
1981	22.6	8.0	18.5
1982	16.2	8.7	16.2
1983	15.9	9.0	15.3
1984	11.8	9.5	10.2
1985	10.3	9.4	8.9
1986	7.4	10.6	8.0
1987	9.0	10.1	5.6
1988	8.8	10.6	4.7

Source: Eurostat

Appendix: Solution of the Taylor contracts model under rational expectations

The model has the form:

$$x_t = bx_{t-1} + dx^e_{t+1} + \gamma(by^e_t + dy^e_{t+1}) + \varepsilon_t$$

$$y_t = \phi(m_t - p_t) + v_t$$

$$m_t = \beta p_t$$

$$p_t = 0.5(x_t + x_{t-1})$$

By substituting the monetary rule into the aggregate demand equation we have

$$y_t = -\delta p_t + v_t$$

where $\delta = \phi(1 - \beta)$.

Substituting this and the equation linking the price level to the current and lagged contracts and taking expectations based on information available at date $t - 1$, we have a difference equation of the form:

$$bx^e_{t-1} - cx^e_t + dx^e_{t+1} = 0$$

where $c = [1 + 0.5\gamma\delta]/[1 - 0.5\gamma\delta]$ (cf. Taylor, 1979, p. 110).

If we assume that the solution consists of a first-order difference equation as below:

$$x^e_t = \alpha x^e_{t-1}$$

then the value of α can be found from the following equation:

101

$$x_{t-1}^e[b - c\alpha + d\alpha^2] = 0$$

There are two values of α which satisfy this equation but one will typically be greater than unity, and so, for stability, it is necessary to assume that this root plays no role in the adjustment of x. We therefore set α equal to the smaller of the two roots:

$$\alpha = \frac{c - \sqrt{c^2 - 4d(1 - d)}}{2d}$$

The expected value of x_{t-1} at $t - 1$ equals the actual value and the actual value of x_t equals its expected value at date $t - 1$ plus the random disturbance term ε_t, so we can write the following equation for the contract:

$$x_t = \alpha x_{t-1} + \varepsilon_t$$

and, combining this with the equation for the price level, we have:

$$p_t = \alpha p_{t-1} + 0.5(\varepsilon_t + \varepsilon_{t-1})$$

Thus the price level follows an ARMA(1,1) process. This has the interesting property that a shock to the price level may have effects that build up over several periods in that the maximum effect will occur two periods after the actual disturbance has taken place. This conforms to the type of adjustment path to disturbances often observed in real-world economies.

6.
The determinants of consumption and investment expenditures

6.1 The stylized facts of consumption and investment

In this chapter we take a close look at the determinants of two of the most important categories of expenditure within total GDP—the levels of consumption and investment expenditures. Over the last 30 years consumption expenditures have accounted for an average of around 60 per cent of GDP while investment, as measured by Gross Domestic Fixed Capital Formation (GDFCF), has accounted for around 19 per cent. Hence an understanding of the factors which influence both these categories of expenditure is of key importance to a macroeconomist.

Consumption and investment differ noticeably in their relationship with GDP. In terms of its time-series properties, consumption is considerably less erratic than GDP, while the reverse is true for GDFCF. These properties are illustrated in Figs 6.1 and 6.2. In Fig. 6.1 we see the logarithms of consumption and GDP over the period 1960–88. It is evident that the responses of the two series to the two major recessions, in 1975 and 1980, are quite different. GDP shows an actual downturn in both cases while consumption merely flattens out. When we turn to a similar diagram for GDFCF and GDP we see a very different pattern. The downturns in GDFCF are much greater than those in GDP, that in 1980 being particularly striking.

It is this difference between the behaviour of consumption and investment expenditures which constitutes the main stylized fact that our theory must

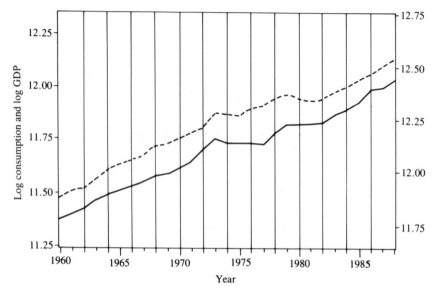

Figure 6.1 Real consumption (———) and real GDP (–––), 1960–88 (log scale). (*Source:* Eurostat)

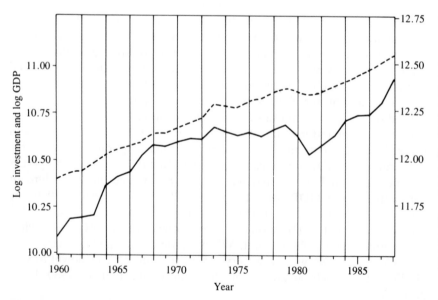

Figure 6.2 Real gross domestic fixed capital formation (———) and real GDP (–––), 1960–88 (log scale). (*Source:* Eurostat)

seek to explain. The theories of consumption and investment which we examine in the following sections seek to use the principles of utility and profit maximization to explain the relative smoothness of consumption and the relative volatility of investment.

6.2 The theory of household consumption choice

Consider an economy containing a large number of identical households. We will discuss the behaviour of a single representative household, which makes a choice between consumption in the present, C_1, and consumption in the future, C_2 (for simplicity, we refer to the present and the future as periods 1 and 2). Our household receives income M_1 and M_2 in periods 1 and 2, respectively, and is free to borrow or lend at the going market rate of interest, r, providing that its borrowing plan is consistent with its intertemporal budget constraint. This constraint is specified in the following equation, which shows the maximization problem facing the household:

$$\text{Max } U(C_1,C_2) \tag{6.1}$$

subject to

$$C_1 + C_2/(1 + r) = M_1 + M_2/(1 + r)$$

The second part of this expression is the intertemporal budget constraint. It states that the present value of current plus future consumption expenditures must equal the present value of current plus future income. To be consistent with this constraint, a household planning to borrow in the current period must simultaneously plan to consume less than its income in the future.

To analyse this problem, let us turn to a graphical representation. Figure 6.3 illustrates our model. The optimal consumption plan is found by searching for a tangency between the one of the household's indifference curves and its budget line. The budget line is easily found by joining the extreme points in which all consumption takes place in period 1, in which case $C_1 = M_1 + M_2/(1 + r)$, and in which all consumption takes place in period 2, in which case $C_2 = M_2 + M_1(1 + r)$. Thus the slope of the budget line is equal to $-(1 + r)$, i.e. sacrificing one unit of consumption in period 1 enables consumption in period 2 to be increased by one unit plus the rate of interest. The slope of the household's indifference curve shows its marginal rate of substitution between current and future income, i.e. the increase in future consumption necessary to compensate the household for a marginal decrease in its current consumption. Hence the optimum point, at which the indifference curve and the budget line are tangential to each other, represents a state in which the value put on trading off current and future consumption by the household (the marginal rate of substitution) is

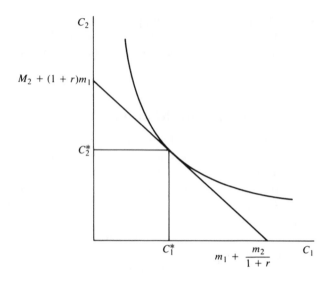

Figure 6.3 Optimum consumption in the two-period model

equal to the trade-off available to it through the loan market (the rate of interest). The optimum solution for the household is therefore to choose consumption level C_1^* in period one and C_2^* in period 2.

Analysis of the above model indicates that, for a given set of household preferences, there are three important factors determining optimal consumption expenditures. These are the level of current income, the level of future income and the rate of interest. Taken together, they determine the lifetime wealth of the household which in turn defines its budget constraint and its consumption choice. In the early analysis of consumption behaviour by Keynes the level of current income was given the major role in determining current consumption expenditures, but this analysis suggests that this is misleading. Current income is only important in so far as it affects the present value of lifetime wealth. If the household expects to live for a long time then M_2 will be very large relative to M_1 and therefore quite large changes in current income will have very small effects on current consumption. Hence the idea that there is a mechanical linkage between variations in current consumption and current income is not consistent with the intertemporal choice model of consumption behaviour.

Another way of expressing the same point is to note that there are an infinite number of different combinations of M_1 and M_2 which can give rise to the budget constraint shown in Fig. 6.1. However, the specific time pattern of income is unimportant in determining the optimal consumption choice: all that matters is the position of the budget line.

Let us consider two very extreme cases to illustrate this point. First, suppose our household wins the football pools in period 1 and promptly decides to retire from the labour market and live off its good fortune. In this case, M_1 is large while M_2 is zero, but it is clearly in the interests of the household to use the loans market to smooth out its consumption path relative to the pattern of income receipts. Now consider a household with no income in the current period but which expects to receive a substantial bequest in the future. Such a household will find it optimal to borrow against its future income in order to finance some consumption in the current period. Again, the household is using the loans market to smooth out its consumption pattern relative to its income pattern. Therefore when an effective loan market exists, the specific time pattern of income receipts is irrelevant. The household uses the loan market to redistribute its consumption through time in order to maximize utility.

The fact that in this model households choose to smooth out consumption expenditures relative to fluctuations in their income illustrates its usefulness in explaining one of the key stylized facts noted in Sec. 6.1. Suppose that households view recessions as essentially temporary phenomena. In such circumstances they will not cut consumption in line with a recession in GDP. Thus we would expect to see a somewhat smoother time path of consumption expenditure relative to that of GDP. Alternatively, we would expect to see the ratio of consumption expenditures to GDP rise in a recession but fall in a boom.

6.3 Extensions of the household consumption model

In the previous section we looked at the basic model of intertemporal consumption choice by a representative household. We found that the existence of an effective market for loans enabled the household to smooth out its consumption through time in order to maximize utility. This tends to weaken the link between current consumption and current income which has traditionally formed a central part of Keynesian macroeconomic thinking. Given the importance of the existence of the market for loans, it is important to consider what might happen if this market is not present or if there exist significant imperfections within it.

The most frequently observed imperfection in the market for loans is the inability of agents to borrow against future income. There are a number of plausible economic reasons why this might occur. For example, in most cases individual agents have much better information about their future income possibilities than do lending institutions. Trying to convince one's bank manager that our cash flow position will improve significantly in the near future is a position in which many of us find ourselves at some stage of

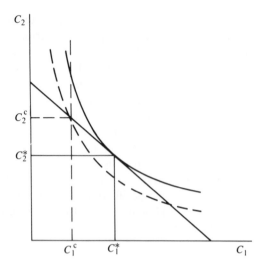

Figure 6.4 Consumption in the two-period model with liquidity constraints

our lives. The point is that, when it is difficult to convince lenders that they will be repaid with a reasonable degree of certainty, the supply side of the loans market may simply fail to materialize.

To illustrate the problems that constraints on the supply side of the loans market may create we again turn to a graphical analysis. Figure 6.4 shows the intertemporal choice facing the same household we analysed in Fig. 6.3. However, this time there is an extra constraint imposed on the household in that we will not allow it to borrow against future income in order to finance current consumption. This constraint is indicated in the figure by the broken vertical line along which $C_1 = M_1$. Let us now consider the relationship between this constraint and the optimal choice of the household. If the unconstrained optimal choice implied $C_1^* < M_1$ then the extra constraint is irrelevant, i.e. it fails to bite. In such circumstances the household can achieve its first-best consumption plan. However, this is not the situation depicted in the figure, which shows a household that wants to consume more than its current income within the current time period. The best that can be achieved in such a situation is for the household to consume all its current income in period 1 and all its future income in period 2. In other words, the absence of an effective supply side to the loans market has removed the possibility of increasing utility through consumption smoothing. Since our household cannot achieve its first-best consumption plan there is necessarily a reduction in utility. This is indicated in the figure by the broken indifference curve, which shows the maximum level of utility available, given the constraints on borrowing.

We have seen that, when there are biting liquidity constraints, the household's utility is lower than it would be if there was an effective loans market. However, there is another important implication of the liquidity-constrained model in that it restores the linkage between current income and current consumption which is emphasized so strongly in Keynesian theory. In the circumstances illustrated by Fig. 6.2 the distribution of income receipts is important in determining the pattern of consumption. Suppose, for example, that current income rises and future income falls in such a way as to leave the present value of lifetime wealth unaltered. In the unconstrained model there would be no effect on the level of consumption, either in the present or in the future. This contrasts sharply with the liquidity-constrained model in which the redistribution of income through time represents a relaxation of the constraint on the household's current level of consumption. The rise in current income is matched fully by a rise in consumption, unless the rise in income is sufficiently great to cause the liquidity constraint to cease to bite. Therefore, if a household is liquidity constrained we are likely to observe a much closer linkage between movements in its current income and consumption than if it had free access to the loans market.

It is worth considering at this stage the circumstances under which liquidity constraints might become important. At any particular time there is likely to be a mixture of constrained and unconstrained households in the economy. It is also likely, however, that the relative size of the two groups will vary with the state of the business cycle. During a boom, incomes are high and rising, and therefore fewer households will see their current consumption levels as being constrained by their current income. In contrast, during a recession, incomes are low and falling, and households may therefore wish to borrow against their future income in order to maintain consumption levels during what they see as a temporary fall in income. Despite this, it is frequently observed that credit market conditions are relatively tight during recessions, with loans being much harder to obtain than during booms. This is particularly the case for individuals who become unemployed with no certain prospects of obtaining alternative employment in the near future. Banks may reasonably be suspicious of extending loans to finance current consumption in these circumstances. Thus the degree to which the household sector is liquidity constrained is likely to rise during a recession. Again we see that the Keynesian approach to the macroeconomy seems to gain in relevance in economies which are experiencing a recession.

The second extension of the consumption model which we will consider is the impact of government borrowing on households' decisions. Let us consider a case in which the government decides to finance its current expenditure by issuing bonds rather than by raising taxes. This has the effect of raising the current disposable income of the household sector. However, there is clearly an offsetting effect on future disposable income, since at some later date the government must raise taxes in order to redeem the bonds it has issued. If there is an effective loans market then it can easily be seen that this will have no effect on the typical household's consumption choices. Current disposable income rises by an amount τ equal to the value of the taxes which would have been levied had the government not resorted to borrowing. This is exactly offset by the fall in disposable income equal to $(1 + r)\tau$ in period 2, which is equal to the taxes levied in the second period to pay off the nominal value of the debt incurred in the first period, plus interest. Although the pattern of income receipts has changed, the present value of lifetime wealth has not, and so there is no reason for the household to change its consumption plans. This argument is often referred to as the *Ricardian equivalence proposition*, since it was first put forward by the eighteenth-century economist, David Ricardo. Another way of thinking of the point being argued here is that current debt and future taxes are regarded as being equivalent to each other by the household sector.

Although the Ricardian equivalence proposition clearly holds in the simple model we have put forward here, it is possible to argue that relaxation of any one of a variety of strong assumptions underlying the model may cause it to break down. Consider first the assumption that there is an effective loans market. We have already seen that in the presence of liquidity constraints the pattern of income receipts through time does influence the level of current consumption expenditures. It therefore follows that when there are liquidity constraints Ricardian equivalence cannot hold. By reducing current taxes and increasing current disposable income the issuing of government debt acts as a substitute for the missing market in loans, permitting households to expand their current consumption. Moreover, since the household sector is more likely to be subject to liquidity constraints during a recession, it follows that a bond-financed deficit may succeed in stimulating consumption expenditures in these circumstances where it might fail to do so during a boom.

The second qualification to the Ricardian equivalence proposition to which we need to draw attention concerns the situation in which the taxes needed to redeem the bonds issued, plus the interest on these bonds, fall outside the lifetime of the households who gain the benefit of the lower taxes. This might at first seem an obvious reason why consumption expenditures may be stimulated by the temporarily lower taxes, but it neglects the possibility that the actions of the current generation may be affected by their concern for the welfare of future generations. Barro (1974) has argued that if the utility of the next generation enters the utility function of the current generation then Ricardian equivalence holds, even when taxes are levied after the current generation has died. In reply to this, Tobin (1980) has pointed out that this assumes that all members of the current generation care about the utility of the next generation, while, in practice, we find it difficult to think of good reasons why childless households should do so. Thus, despite Barro's spirited defence of the Ricardian equivalence proposition, there are still important reasons why we should treat it with more than a pinch of scepticism.

6.4 The theory of investment decisions

In analysing the determination of investment expenditures at the macroeconomic level we begin in the same way as with the consumption function. Taking a single representative agent, we analyse the determinants of desired investment for that agent and then aggregate up to analyse the determinants of investment for the economy as a whole.

Investment can take a number of different forms. The most usual division is between investment in physical capital for production and additions to the stock of housing and to stocks of finished products for later sale and consumption. We will concentrate mainly on the first of these categories, i.e. the decision by firms to purchase plant and machinery to be used in the productive process. However, much of the discussion of this topic also applies to the other two categories of investment.

When we describe the firm's investment decision we must take into account two important stages:

1. Given any particular set of external factors, what level of capital would the firm wish to employ?
2. Given that it is costly to change the stock of capital quickly, how much extra capital will a firm choose to purchase in any given time period?

The first stage of the decision process involves a straightforward static optimization problem. However, the second requires a more dynamic analysis in which time enters explicitly. Despite the fact that the two decisions are closely related, and will usually be taken simultaneously in practice, this division is a very useful one for expositional purposes, and we will make use of it below.

Let us first consider stage 1, the determination of the optimal level of the capital stock. This decision can be framed in standard microeconomic terms. Firms are assumed to choose capital as one of a range of possible factors of production in order to maximize profit. Therefore a firm will choose a level of capital input at which the marginal return to employing capital, in terms of profitability, equals the marginal cost of employing capital. Suppose the firm under consideration is a perfect competitor. This

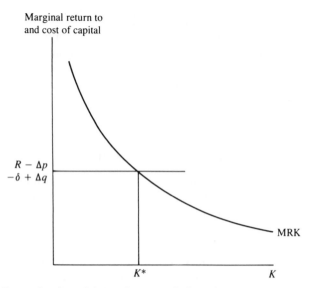

Figure 6.5 Determination of the optimum capital stock

means that the marginal return to employing capital is equal to the marginal product of capital, as given by the production function. If we further assume that the production function exhibits diminishing returns to individual factors, then we can reasonably conclude that the marginal return to employing capital declines as the level of capital input increases. This is shown in the downward-sloping locus MRK in Fig. 6.5. The structure of tax incentives for physical investment is also important in determining the return to holding capital. This feature is an important institutional characteristic of most industrial countries in which governments have frequently made use of differential tax rates on holdings of physical and financial assets in order to stimulate investment and therefore productive potential. In terms of the figure, a more generous treatment of physical capital will shift the MRK curve outwards.

The marginal cost of purchasing physical capital consists of the opportunity cost of holding such capital rather than holding financial assets. This in turn is determined by the following factors:

1. The real rate of return available from holding financial assets. This can be written $R - \Delta p$, where R is the nominal rate of interest and Δp is the rate of inflation.
2. The rate of depreciation of physical capital. We will assume that depreciation takes place at a constant exponential rate of δ per cent of the outstanding capital stock per time period.

3. The change in the price of capital goods relative to other goods. If capital is expected to appreciate in value then this will increase the return on holding capital goods, irrespective of their productivity in terms of the output of consumer goods. This last term is written Δq.

Since all three of the factors listed above are exogenous for the individual firm, we represent the marginal cost of capital function as a horizontal line in Fig. 6.5.

The optimal capital input is now determined by the intersection of the marginal return to capital schedule (MRK) and the horizontal marginal cost of capital line. The profit-maximizing level of capital input can be disturbed because of shifts to either locus. In particular, government policy can alter the level of capital input by giving a more favourable tax treatment to earnings from this source, and therefore shifting the MRK locus outwards. Alternatively, the government can operate through the financial markets to stimulate investment by lowering interest rates, and therefore shifting the marginal cost of capital line downwards.

We have concentrated so far solely on the determination of the profit-maximizing level of capital input in a purely static sense. In other words, we have ignored the fact that adjustment is likely to be costly, and therefore the investment necessary to increase capital input will be spread over a number of time periods. The simplest type of cost of adjustment to incorporate into our model is the quadratic cost function.

Suppose we specify costs as follows:

$$C_t = \gamma_1(K_t - K_t^*)^2 + \gamma_2(K_t - K_{t-1})^2 \qquad (6.2)$$

This equation splits costs up into two components. The first of these is the cost involved in having a capital input which differs from the static optimum. The second is the cost of changing the level of the capital input over its value in the previous period. Both types of cost take on a quadratic functional form. Differentiating Eq. (6.2) with respect to K_t and setting the derivative equal to zero enables us to solve for the level of capital which minimizes the above cost function. A little rearranging of the first-order condition yields the following expression:

$$K_t - K_{t-1} = [\gamma_1/(\gamma_1 + \gamma_2)](K_t^* - K_{t-1}) \qquad (6.3)$$

which states that the change in the capital input is some fraction of the difference between the static optimum capital input and the value in the previous period. This formulation is familiar in applied econometrics as the *partial adjustment model*, with the term in square brackets being the partial adjustment parameter, i.e. that fraction of any deviation from equilibrium which is eliminated within the current time period. Note that it is only in the special case in which there are no costs to adjusting the capital input (i.e. when $\gamma_2 = 0$) that full adjustment to the static equilibrium takes place within a single time period.

One factor to which we need to draw attention is that all the discussion so far has concentrated on the determination of the firm's choice of capital input. This is different from the capital stock which the firm has in place, since the degree of intensity with which capital can be employed can be varied. In practice, it is very difficult to measure the input of capital services directly and empirical analyses are often conducted using the capital stock as the endogenous variable. Nevertheless, despite the empirical difficulties, there is a clear conceptual difference here which should be borne in mind when interpreting estimates of this model.

Unit 6.1

Estimating the consumption function

Obtaining reliable estimates of the parameters of the consumption function is an important part of macroeconomic modelling, since consumption constitutes the largest element of total expenditure. For many years the main problem involved in getting such estimates has been to allow for the fact that the response of consumption to a change in income is not instantaneous. Consumers typically spread their response to an increase in disposable income over a number of time periods, because it is either costly in some way to adjust too rapidly or it takes time for changes in current income to be incorporated into their estimates of permanent income. Many alternative formulations have been put forward to allow for this phenomenon.

In recent years the most empirically successful form of the consumption function has been that put forward by David Hendry and a variety of co-workers. This has made use of the idea of an *error-correction mechanism* formulation which combines short-run adjustment of consumption to changes in income with a specification which ensures that, in the long run, the ratio of the two variables converges on a fixed value. This is achieved by estimating a regression equation which relates changes in consumption to changes in income, to allow for the short-run relationship between the two variables, but which also includes terms in the levels of the two variables, which allows for the existence of a long-run relationship between them.

A typical example of the Hendry type of equation is given below. This equation is taken from the Davidson, Hendry, Srba and Yeo (DHSY) (1978) consumption paper, which is widely regarded as one of the seminal pieces of work on the subject. The equation is estimated using quarterly data over the period 1958:Q1 to 1975:Q4:

$$\Delta_4 c_t = \underset{(0.03)}{0.48\Delta_4 y_t} - \underset{(0.04)}{0.23\Delta_1\Delta_4 y_t} - \underset{(0.01)}{0.09(c - y)_{t-4}} + \underset{(0.002)}{0.006 DUM} -$$

$$\underset{(0.02)}{0.12\Delta_4 p_t} - \underset{(0.10)}{0.31\Delta_1\Delta_4 p_t}$$

$$(U6.1.1)$$

$$R^2 = 0.85 \qquad DW = 2.0 \qquad \hat{\sigma} = 0.0062$$

Standard errors are in parentheses below the coefficients. *DUM* is a dummy variable included to capture the effects of periods in which changes in indirect tax rates were widely anticipated. *c* and *y* are the logarithms of real consumers' expenditure on non-durable goods and services and real personal disposable income, respectively.

The Δ_4 terms indicate fourth-order differencing, i.e. the change of the variable in question relative to its value in the same quarter of the preceding year. Hence, the coefficient on $\Delta_4 y_t$ of 0.48 indicates that a 1 per cent change in disposable income will produce a 0.48 per cent change in consumption within the same year, i.e. the *short-run income elasticity of consumption* is equal to 0.48. The inclusion of the $\Delta_1 \Delta_4 y$ term shows that it matters whether the growth rate of income is rising or falling. In periods when income growth is rising the negative coefficient on this variable indicates that consumption is, to some extent, lagging behind. Similarly, the negative coefficient on $\Delta_4 p$ indicates that inflation affects consumption negatively and the negative coefficient on $\Delta_1 \Delta_4 p$ shows that when inflation is rising this further reduces consumption. It is the inclusion of the levels term $(c - y)_{t-4}$ which ensures that the model has a long-run solution. If all variables concerned are growing at a constant rate then the inclusion of this term implies that consumption and income must approach some steady-state ratio in the long run. The negative sign of the coefficient on this variable shows that when this long-run ratio is exceeded there is a tendency for consumption expenditures to fall.

Equations of this type have provided a theoretically reasonable and empirically convincing explanation of consumption expenditures over a number of years. However, there is evidence from the late 1980s that this specification has not been very successful in explaining the significant rise in consumption expenditure and in the consumption income ratio which took place. Attempts have been made to revise the model to allow for other effects such as changes in the demographic structure of the population and in the value of the housing stock.

Unit 6.2

The *Q* theory of investment

A popular empirical model of investment has resulted from a paper by Tobin (1969). This argues that an important determinant of investment is the relationship between the market value of a firm and the replacement cost of its physical assets. Suppose we write the following:

$$Q = MV/RK \qquad \text{(U6.2.1)}$$

where *MV* is the market value of the firm and *RK* is the replacement cost of capital. *Q*-theory hypothesizes that the level of investment undertaken by the firm will be positively related to the value of *Q*. Alternatively, when the market value of the firm rises relative to the replacement cost of its physical assets it becomes more desirable for the firm to increase the stock of physical assets it holds.

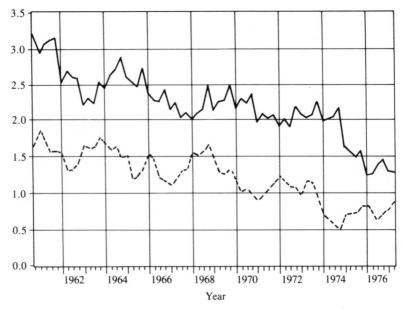

Figure U6.2.1 Investment (———) and Q (- - -) 1960: Q4 to 1977: Q2

We can put the Q-theory on a firmer microeconomic footing as follows. First we note that the market value of the firm equals the discounted present value of its future profit stream, i.e.:

$$MV = \int_0^\infty \pi e^{-\rho t} = \pi/\rho \tag{U6.2.2}$$

where a constant stream of profits and a discount rate for the firm equal to ρ is assumed. The coefficient ρ can also be interpreted as the cost of capital facing the firm. Second, note that the rate of return on the firm's current physical assets, δ, is implicitly defined as that rate of discount which makes the value of the stream of future profits just equal to the value of the firm's physical assets:

$$RK = \pi/\delta \tag{U6.2.3}$$

Putting these two equations together yields an expression for Q of the form $Q = \delta/\rho$. If we now write investment as a positively sloped function of Q, $I = I(Q)$, where $I'(.) > 0$, then this can easily be related to the investment function in the main text in that it simply states that investment will take place if the return on physical capital is high relative to the firm's discount rate (or its cost of capital).

The advantage of Q-theory lies not in its theoretical novelty but in its empirical applications. It is hard in practice to obtain good empirical measures of firms' rates of return and almost impossible to observe firms' discount rates. However, the Q-ratio is easily computable and therefore a natural candidate for inclusion in empirical investment equations.

An application of the Q investment model to the UK Industrial and Commercial Companies Sector has been provided by Oulton (1981). Figure U6.2.1 shows Oulton's data for investment in this sector as a percentage of their outstanding stock of physical assets. Visual inspection suggests that the two series are closely related to each other, but the presence of a common trend means that this may be unreliable. A more formal test of the existence of a relationship between the two can be obtained by using the augmented Dickey–Fuller (ADF) test for the existence of a co-integrating relationship. Application of this test yields an ADF statistic of -4.56, which is greater in absolute value than the 95 per cent critical value of -3.94. Thus we may conclude that the apparent relationship between the two series is not spurious in that there is clear evidence that they move together through time.

Review questions

1. Suppose a household begins with an endowment of financial assets worth £500 and receives an annual income of a further £1000. If the rate of interest equals 5 per cent, and assuming that the household lives for ever, compute the present value of the household's resources. What level of consumption can be sustained without reducing the value household wealth?

2. Consider an economy in which the demand for capital goods is proportional to the level of output according to the formula:

$$K = 3Y$$

and adjustment costs for capital are given by the following partial adjustment formula:

$$C_t = (K_t - K_t^*)^2 + (K_t - K_{t-1})^2$$

Derive the investment function for this economy and illustrate the time path of investment in response to an increase in the level of output.

3. Discuss the role of liquidity constraints in generating a link between aggregate consumption expenditure and current disposable income.

4. Using the Q approach to investment decisions, show how the behaviour of the stock market can affect investment and, through it, the behaviour of the real economy.

7.
The monetary sector

7.1 Interest rates and the velocity of circulation

One of the most important theoretical features of the demand for money function is its dependence on the rate of interest. Models which generate such a dependence will be discussed in Secs 7.2 and 7.3. The purpose of this section, however, is to provide some empirical motivation for the theoretical analysis. Perhaps the most striking example of the relationship between the demand for money and the rate of interest is provided in Fig. 7.1, taken from Artis and Lewis (1984). This shows the scatter diagram of the long-term rate of interest against the inverse of the velocity of circulation for over sixty annual observations. It is easy to see that the points are grouped

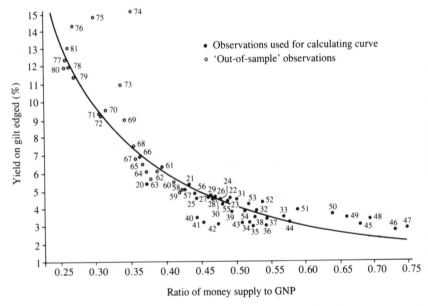

Figure 7.1 Interest rates and the demand for money, 1920–81. (*Source:* Artis and Lewis, 1984)

remarkably closely around a non-linear functional form. Thus the existence of a negative relationship between the demand for money and the rate of interest is given striking confirmation by the data. In the following sections we discuss the economic reasons why this might be the case.

7.2 The inventory theory approach to the demand for money

One of the earliest attempts to provide a suitable microeconomic foundation for the theory of the demand for money was provided by Baumol in 1952. This theory centres on the transactions demand for money and shows how such a demand can be derived from the principles of inventory management. A transactions demand for money arises because of the need for some asset to serve as a medium of exchange in order to smooth the process of trade between agents. Although paper money, and, latterly, current accounts with the banks, have traditionally provided this, the pace of financial innovation has increased remarkably in recent years and it is becoming more difficult to define just what constitutes money. The problem facing each agent in the Baumol model is how to minimize the opportunity cost of holding the barren asset (money) in terms of the interest foregone by not holding other assets, while maintaining a level of money balances sufficient to finance the stream of transactions the agent makes.

Inventory management is a useful way of thinking about the demand for money because of the difference between the pattern of income receipts and expenditures through time. A typical household receives income in discrete lumps at fixed intervals of time (for example, a weekly wage bill or a monthly salary cheque). In contrast, expenditures take place more or less continuously through time. This creates the opportunity for the household to manage its money holdings so as to earn some interest on that fraction of its income which is not needed to finance purchases at any particular point in time.

Let us now move to a formal model of the demand for money based on the principles we have described. Consider a household which receives a fixed amount of income, Y, at fixed intervals of time. We will assume, for simplicity, that all this income is spent during the interval between income receipts, so that the net money balance held immediately before the receipt is always zero. The household has the choice of holding its income in a non-interest-bearing chequeing account, which can be used to finance transactions expenditures, or in the form of interest-bearing bonds, which cannot be used in transactions. Clearly, the best strategy is for the household to hold part of its income in the form of bonds and retain part as money to finance expenditure. Since expenditures take place continuously, there will

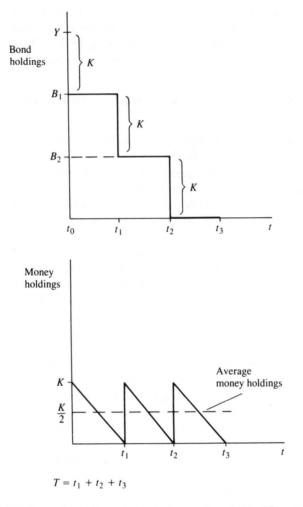

Figure 7.2 The Baumol–Tobin model of the transaction demand for money

come a time when the household must transform some fraction of its bond holdings into money in order to finance further transactions. Each time it does this we assume that it incurs a fixed cost in the form of a broker's fee, or a bank charge, for making the transfer. Thus there is a trade-off between the opportunity cost of holding money, in terms of the interest foregone, and the brokerage cost of making frequent transfers between bonds and money.

A stylized version of the time path of money and bond holdings is illustrated in Fig. 7.2. At time t_0 the agent receives income equal to Y. K units of this is retained as money and B_1 units is used to purchase bonds. Money holdings are then run down until they reach zero at time t_1, at which time the household makes a transfer of size K from bonds to money. Bond holdings therefore fall to B_2 while money holdings are restored to K. Once again, money holdings are run down to finance expenditures until at time t_2 they are zero. At this time the agent transfers the balance of his or her bond holdings into money and runs this balance down until the end of the period, at which time a new income receipt will be forthcoming.

The agent's problem can be set in a simple mathematical form as follows. First, we write the cost function for managing the portfolio as:

$$C = bY/K + rK/2 \qquad (7.1)$$

where C is the total cost, b is the brokerage fee for making a transfer, Y is total income for the period, K is the size of the transfer made each time the household makes a shift from bonds into money and r is the interest rate on bonds. The first part of the cost-function expression gives the total brokerage charges, since Y/K equals the number of transfers made during the period. The second part gives the opportunity cost of holding money, since $K/2$ equals the average level of money holdings during the period.

When written in this form, the household's problem has a straightforward mathematical solution. To minimize cost it must choose a value of K, the size of each transfer, such that the first derivative of Eq. (7.1) with respect to K equals zero. Thus we require:

$$dC/dK = -bY/K^2 + r/2 = 0 \quad \text{or} \quad K = \sqrt{2b}\, Y/r \qquad (7.2)$$

It is probable that the solution will not yield an integer value for the number of trips to the bank. However, the optimal number can be found easily by taking the integer value closest to the solution.

Since average money holdings equal half the size of the transfer made, we therefore have a demand for money function of the form:

$$M = \alpha\sqrt{Y/r} \qquad (7.3)$$

where $\alpha = 0.5\sqrt{2b}$. The demand for money therefore depends on three main factors. These are the size of each period's income receipt, the rate of interest available on alternative assets and the brokerage charge payable for making transfers between money and bonds. In addition, we can make the following points about the responsiveness of money demand to each of these factors:

1. Since the demand for money is related to the square root of income Y it
   follows that the income elasticity of demand for money will be equal to

0.5. This is somewhat lower than the estimates obtained in many empirical studies (which tend to be about 1.0). However, it may be the case that these empirical studies use a definition of money which is too broad to capture the pure transactions demand.

2. The rate of interest enters with an elasticity of -0.5. This represents an extension of the simple transactions demand model presented in many elementary texts in which the rate of interest is ignored. Note, however, that the presence of the rate of interest has nothing to do with the relative riskiness of holding bonds and money, or with the possibility of making capital gains by shifting between the two.

3. A reduction in the brokerage fee for making transfers (b) will reduce the demand for money. This is because it will become cheaper for households to make more frequent transfers and therefore economize their holdings of the barren asset, money. Such a reduction might come about because of an increase in competition between banks, or because of an improvement in banking technology such as the introduction of computer transfers.

7.3 The asset demand for money

The inventory approach to the demand for money focuses on the role of money as a medium for financing transactions. However, there is also a need to consider a second motive for holding money—as one of a range of financial assets used as a store of wealth. An obvious point here is why agents would wish to hold wealth as money when there are alternative assets which bear a higher rate of return in the form of interest. The answer to this is that it is only when we allow for the fact that other types of financial assets such as bonds can fluctuate in value that it becomes possible to think of rational agents choosing to hold their wealth in the form of money. In a riskless world no-one would choose to hold their wealth in this form.

Tobin (1956) provides a theory of the demand for money as one of a portfolio of assets making up financial wealth. For simplicity, let us assume that there are only two types of asset: money which bears no interest but is fixed in value, and bonds which bear interest but which can vary in terms of value. Again, the problem facing agents is a trade-off, this time between the high return obtainable by holding a large fraction of their wealth in terms of bonds and the risk which this strategy necessarily entails. A demand for money therefore arises in this situation because of the relative safety it offers in comparison with other assets.

To look further at the Tobin model, let us turn to Fig. 7.3. The representative agent has an initial stock of wealth which he or she wishes to distribute

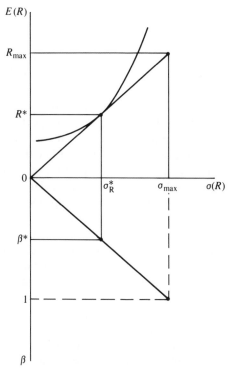

Figure 7.3 The Tobin portfolio model

between money and bonds so as to maximize utility. Utility is increasing in the expected return on the portfolio $E(R)$ and decreasing in the riskiness of the portfolio $\sigma(R)$. Our agent's preferences are represented by a family of convex indifference curves, one of which is shown in the figure. The budget line, or set of available trade-offs, is shown by the upward-sloping straight line and is determined as follows. First, if all wealth is held as money, the portfolio bears zero return and attracts no risk, and the origin must therefore lie on the budget line. Second, the other end point can be determined by asking what will happen if all the portfolio is held as bonds, which determines the point of maximum expected return and maximum risk (R_{max} and σ_{max}, respectively). The budget line is then obtained by joining these two extreme points.

Assuming that the agent has well-behaved preferences, i.e. that he or she dislikes risk sufficiently to generate an adequate degree of convexity in the indifference curves, then the equilibrium will be of the type shown in Fig. 7.3 as the tangency between the indifference curve and the budget line. This shows the utility-maximizing expected return, R^*, and the utility-maximizing level of risk, σ^*. Since the expected return is less than could be obtained by holding all the portfolio in the form of bonds, it follows that part of it is held as money.

The determination of the division of the portfolio between money and bonds is shown by the lower part of Fig. 7.3, where β is the fraction of the portfolio held as bonds. Obviously, at the origin β is zero, since this corresponds to the point of zero expected return and hence all the portfolio is held as money. At the opposite extreme, when the portfolio has maximum risk, σ_{max}, it follows that β must be one, i.e. all the portfolio is held as bonds. If we join these two extremes by a straight line then we can show the determination of the utility-maximizing proportion of bonds as a function of the utility-maximizing level of risk. In our particular case, since the agent chooses a level of risk σ^*, it follows that β^* is the proportion of total wealth held as bonds.

The analysis so far shows that the asset demand for money depends on three main factors: the value of the initial stock of wealth, the rate of interest on bonds and the riskiness of holding bonds. It is possible to consider the implications of changes in any of these three factors for money demand. The effect of an increase in wealth is the easiest to deal with. Since the portfolio is split between money and bonds it follows that an increase in the stock of wealth will increase holdings of both.

Changes in the rate of interest and the level of riskiness are somewhat more ambiguous in their effects. Consider first the effects of an increase in the rate of interest as shown in Fig. 7.4. When interest rates rise the budget line shifts upwards to the broken line shown in the figure. The equilibrium point shifts from A to B and the new risk–return combination is given by $R^{*'}$, $\sigma^{*'}$. As drawn, the agent chooses both a higher level of return and risk in the new portfolio and therefore the proportion held as bonds must have increased. This is shown in the lower part of the figure by the increase in β from β^* to $\beta^{*'}$. Thus the increase in the rate of interest is shown as reducing the demand for money, while increasing the demand for bonds. However the move from position A to position B is the result of a combination of substitution and income effects. We have implicitly assumed that the substitution effect of higher interest rates is sufficient to offset any possible negative income effect on the proportion of the portfolio held as bonds. It is, however, possible that agents would take advantage of the higher rate of return on bonds to reduce their risk by holding a lower fraction of the portfolio in this form if they were sufficiently risk-averse. Thus there is a possibility in this model that an increase in the rate of interest might have the apparently perverse effect of increasing the demand for money.

Now consider the effects of an increase in the degree of risk as shown in

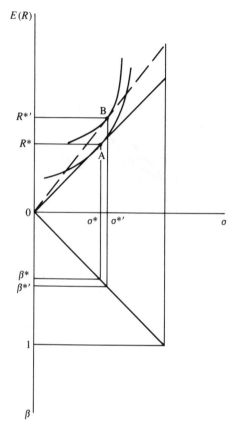

Figure 7.4 Response to an increase in the rate of interest

Fig. 7.5. This produces a shift in the budget constraint to that shown by the broken line and a shift in the equilibrium point from point A to point B. Despite the fact that the degree of risk is higher in the new portfolio ($\sigma^{*\prime}$ rather than σ^*), it does not follow that the agent holds a higher proportion of bonds. This is because the portfolio line shown in the lower part of Fig. 7.5 has also shifted because of the increase in risk. The new line is indicated by a broken line in the lower part and, as drawn, it implies a lower proportion of bonds, and a higher demand for money, in the new portfolio. However, once again, this shift is due to a combination of income and substitution effects, and it is possible, though not very likely, to think of cases in which an increase in the riskiness of bonds could actually reduce the demand for money.

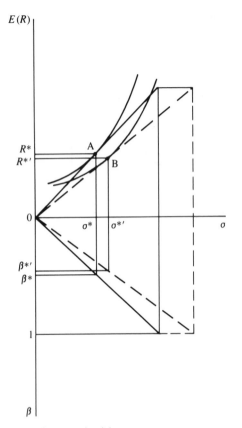

Figure 7.5 Response to an increase in risk

7.4 The determination of the money supply

Our discussion so far has concentrated exclusively on the demand side of the money market. In this section we extend the analysis to deal with the determination of the money stock. The method adopted is based around the *money-multiplier approach*. This derives a relationship between the level of the money stock and the reserves of base money held by the banking system. Since the reserves of the banking system are directly determined by government actions it is often argued that this approach provides a framework for monetary control. However, as we will show, there are a number of problems involved in controlling the money supply through the stock of base money which make such control rather more problematic than it may appear at first sight.

The money-multiplier approach is based on two simple identities. First, we define the stock of money, M, to consist of cash, C, which is defined as notes and coins held outside the central bank, plus bank deposits, D:

$$M \equiv C + D \qquad (7.4)$$

Next, we define the stock of *high-powered* or *base* money, H, to be the sum of cash C and banks' reserves held with the central bank, R:

$$H \equiv C + R \qquad (7.5)$$

If we put these two identities together then a relationship between the total stock of money and the stock of high-powered money can be derived as follows:

$$M = [(1 + c)/(c + r)]H \qquad (7.6)$$

where $c = C/D$ is the *cash–deposit ratio* and $r = R/D$ is the *reserve–deposit ratio*. This equation shows the relationship between the stock of money and the stock of base money for given values of these two ratios. The expression in the square brackets is termed the money multiplier, since it shows the total effect on the stock of money of a unit increase in the monetary base. Since the two components of the stock of base money can be controlled by the monetary policy authorities, it is therefore argued that the money-multiplier relationship provides a means by which the authorities can exercise control over the total money stock.

It is important to remember that the money-multiplier relationship only provides a stable link between total money and the monetary base, if the cash–deposit and reserve–deposit ratios are constant, or at least move in a predictable manner. In practice, this may often fail to be the case, and, under these circumstances, it may not be possible to achieve adequate precision in monetary targeting through this mechanism alone.

Another, specifically British, objection has been put forward to the use of the monetary base method for practical monetary control. In Britain the Bank of England has traditionally taken on the role of the *lender of last resort*. This means that in the event of a run on the deposits of any of the clearing banks the Bank of England will always supply them with the extra reserves needed to stop them failing. The logic behind the central bank adopting this position is that the very knowledge that it will not allow the clearing banks to fail due to a run will be sufficient to prevent a run developing in the first place. However, in order to prevent the clearing banks becoming too reliant on the central bank as a source of funds, the Bank of England reserves the right to charge punitively high interest rates for the provision of this form of short-term liquidity. The problem is that monetary base control requires the authorities to set strict targets for the stock of bank reserves, while the role of lender of last resort requires the

Bank of England to expand reserves on demand. It is the conflict between these goals which has led to objections to the adoption of monetary base control within the British institutional context.

Despite the caveats which have been put forward, the monetary base approach provides a useful framework for thinking about the money-supply process. In particular, it indicates one of the ways in which fiscal and monetary policies may be linked. Suppose the government fails to cover its expenditures by means of taxation. There are two principal methods by which it can cover its deficit. These are by selling financial assets to the non-bank private sector or by borrowing from the banking system. The latter has the effect of increasing the reserves of the banks with the central bank. In other words, it increases the monetary base. Therefore there is a possible link between the government's budget deficit and growth in base money. This link has often been used to argue the case that it is necessary to conduct both a restrictive monetary policy *and* a restrictive fiscal policy in order to achieve a successful disinflation.

Unit 7.1

Estimating the demand for money

Since the demand for money function plays such an important role in macroeconomic modelling it has attracted an enormous amount of interest in the empirical modelling literature. As in the case of the consumption function, a central problem has been to achieve a specification which allows simultaneously for both long- and short-run effects.

One of the key empirical papers on the demand for money in the UK is by Hendry and Mizon (1978). This paper can be regarded as setting the agenda for subsequent research on the topic in much the same way as did Davidson, Hendry, Srba and Yeo (1978) for research into the consumption function. These two papers have much in common in terms of their methodology, since in both cases an error-correction specification is used. The equation estimated therefore allows for a combination of short-run responses to changes in the variables which determine the demand for money and reactions to long-run disequilibrium.

Hendry and Mizon model the demand for broad money in the UK using quarterly data over the period 1963:Q1 to 1975:Q3. Their estimated model takes the form:

$$\Delta(m - p)_t = 1.61 + 0.21\Delta y_t + 0.81\Delta r_t + 0.26\Delta(m - p)_{t-1} - 0.40\Delta p_t$$
$$\quad\quad (0.65)\ (0.09)\quad\ (0.31)\quad\ (0.12)\quad\quad\quad\quad (0.15)$$

$$- 0.23(m - p - y)_{t-1} - 0.61r_{t-4} + 0.14y_{t-4}$$
$$\quad (0.05)\quad\quad\quad\quad\quad (0.21)\quad\ (0.04) \quad\quad\quad\quad\quad\text{(U7.1.1)}$$

$$R^2 = 0.69 \quad\quad \sigma = 0.0091$$

where m, p and y are the natural logarithims of money, the price level and real personal disposable income, respectively, and r is the natural logarithm of one plus the rate of interest. Standard errors are shown in parentheses below the coefficients.

The coefficients on the changes in the logarithms of the exogenous variables show the short-run elasticities of the demand for money in response to changes in these variables. For example, the coefficient on Δy_t indicates that the demand for money increases 2.3 per cent in response to a 10 per cent increase in income within the same quarter. The coefficient on $(m - p - y)_{t-1}$ is a measure of the response of the demand for money to long-run disequilibrium. This variable is the log of the inverse of the velocity of circulation, and thus variations in it measure the deviation from some long-run equilibrium velocity. The coefficient of 0.23 indicates that 23 per cent of any such disequilibrium is eliminated after one quarter. Finally, the positive coefficient on y_{t-4} indicates that the long-run income elasticity of the demand for money is somewhat less than one. This means that the equilibrium velocity of circulation will tend to drift upwards through time as income rises.

Although these estimates appear to be reasonably successful, in both a statistical sense and in terms of their conformity with economic theory, we need to be wary about relying on them to forecast out of the sample period. The monetary sector is notorious for the speed with which innovations, in the form of new types of financial asset, can spread through the markets. Since the data period used for Eq. (U7.1.1) we have seen the building societies enter many of the markets which were previously regarded as the territory of the clearing banks. Hence the monetary aggregate used in demand for money studies has now been broadened to include these institutions. Even allowing for this change, however, there is still evidence to suggest that the demand for money has not been stable through time.

Unit 7.2

How stable is the money multiplier?

In discussing the supply side of the money market we made use of the money-multiplier formula. By using two identities we derive a relationship which states that the stock of money is equal to the product of the money multiplier and the stock of base, or high-powered, money. This can be interpreted as a means of obtaining control of the money supply *providing* that the money multiplier is reasonably stable.

Stability of the money multiplier requires that the ratios of cash to deposits and of bank reserves to deposits both be stable. In practice, these conditions may not be met. As an example, let us consider one of the most famous episodes in monetary history: the monetary contraction that accompanied the 1929 Great Depression in the United States. It is the claim that the Great Depression was the result of inappropriate monetary policy which established Milton Friedman's reputation as the chief proponent of monetarist macroeconomics. It is clearly

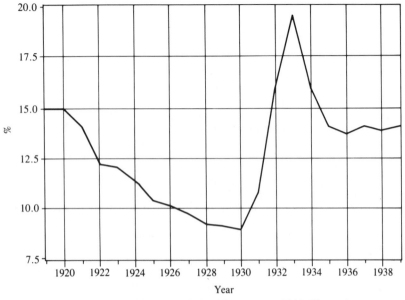

Figure U7.2.1 Cash deposit ratio for US banking system, 1919–39

beyond the scope of this book to provide a definitive answer to such an extensive debate. However, as an example of how it can be potentially misleading to assume a stable money multiplier, this episode has considerable merits.

Before looking in detail at the monetary side of the US economy during this period, it is necessary to consider the broad pattern of events which led up to the Depression. During the 1920s the US economy was booming, output rose fast and unemployment was low. However, by the end of the decade this expansion was becoming unsustainable. One of the by-products of the boom in the real economy had been a rapid rise in the stock market, which reached a peak in 1929. The first signs of trouble in the economy came with the collapse of share prices. This was followed by a collapse of the real economy which led the United States into its deepest ever recession.

Friedman's claim is that the collapse of the real economy was the result of an avoidable mistake on the part of the Federal Reserve System (the US monetary policy authority). Instead of expanding the stock of high-powered money when demand was increasing, it was reduced. This turned what would probably have been a minor downturn in the cycle into a major recession. Whether the initial cause of the recession was monetary or not, there is no doubt that subsequent monetary effects made it worse. Banks began to fail and a panic ensued, leading to a collapse of confidence and spending throughout the economy.

The early 1930s were therefore a period of major monetary upheavals in the United States. It is therefore interesting to examine the behaviour of the components of the money multiplier during this period to see how they were affected by these events. Let us first consider the behaviour of the cash–deposit ratio, which is shown in Fig. U7.2.1. Throughout the 1920s this ratio had

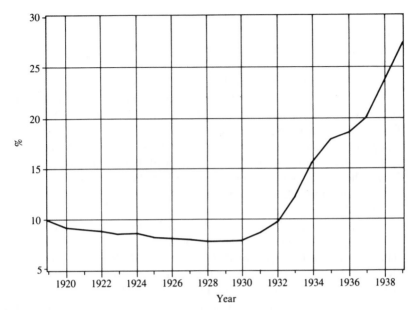

Figure U7.2.2 Reserve deposit ratios for US banking system, 1919–39. (*Source:* Temin, 1976)

declined, but the loss of confidence in the banking system, which was a feature of the recession, led to a large increase in the public's preference for cash rather than bank deposits. Even in 1939, at the end of the period, the public's confidence had not returned sufficiently to restore the cash–deposit ratio to its pre-crash value. A similar story can be told about the reserve–deposit ratio during this period, as shown in Fig. U7.2.2. Having gently declined during the 1920s, this ratio began, and continued, to climb throughout the 1930s as the banks revised upwards their assessment of the riskiness of expanding deposits.

It is obvious from the two figures that the simple money-multiplier formula would be quite misleading in these circumstances. The increase in the two ratios would have had the net effect of reducing the money multiplier considerably. Thus, at a time when monetary expansion was needed to stabilize the economy, the ability of the authorities to engineer an increase in the money stock by increasing base money had been severely weakened.

Review questions

1. A firm receives an income of £10 000 per month, the rate of interest available on invested money is 5 per cent and there is a brokerage charge of £1.60 every time a transfer between money and bonds is made. Use the

Baumol inventory theory to compute the firm's average holdings of money.

2. Consider an economy in which the cash–deposit ratio equals 0.2 and the reserve–deposit ratio equals 0.3. If the central bank issues high-powered money to the value of £1.5 billion, what will be the total value of the money stock in the economy? What will be the effect on the money stock of a government budget deficit of £100 million, 30 per cent of which is financed by borrowing from the central bank?

3. Suppose a crash in the stock market increases the perceived level of riskiness from holding all forms of financial assets other than money. Using the Tobin portfolio model, trace out the effects on the rate of interest and the relative proportions of money and bonds in which agents hold their wealth.

4. Compare and contrast the Baumol inventory approach to the demand for money with Tobin's portfolio approach.

5. The table opposite gives growth rates for real GDP, prices, money and the change in the rate of interest for the French economy. Try plotting real GDP and inflation alongside money growth to see which gives the stronger correlation. If you have access to a computer regression package, try regressing money growth on price and output growth and the change in the interest rate. Do your results look plausible as a demand for money function?

France: Growth rates of GDP, price, money and the interest rate

	GDP	Price	Money M3	Interest rate
1961	5.5	3.4	17.2	−0.5
1962	6.7	4.8	18.7	0.0
1963	5.3	6.3	14.1	0.4
1964	6.5	4.0	9.8	0.7
1965	4.8	2.9	10.9	−0.5
1966	5.2	2.8	10.6	0.6
1967	4.7	3.3	13.1	0.0
1968	4.3	4.4	11.6	1.4
1969	7.0	6.4	6.1	3.1
1970	5.7	5.8	15.3	−0.7
1971	5.4	5.7	18.0	−2.6
1972	5.9	6.1	18.8	−0.7
1973	5.4	7.9	14.7	3.9
1974	3.2	11.0	15.6	3.8
1975	0.2	13.4	18.1	−5.4
1976	5.0	10.1	12.3	1.1
1977	4.6	9.1	14.2	0.4
1978	3.4	10.1	12.4	−1.3
1979	3.2	10.2	14.0	1.9
1980	1.6	11.4	9.7	2.3
1981	1.2	11.4	11.0	3.3
1982	2.5	11.7	11.4	−0.7
1983	0.7	9.8	11.5	−2.1
1984	1.4	7.4	9.5	−0.8
1985	1.7	5.8	6.8	−1.8
1986	2.1	4.6	6.3	−2.2
1987	2.2	2.6	7.3	0.6
1988	2.3	2.8	7.3	−0.4

Source: Eurostat

8.
The macroeconomics of the open economy

8.1 The role of the overseas sector

In this chapter we will examine the role of the overseas sector in the determination of macroeconomic equilibrium. Two important features of this sector are:

1. It introduces a new source of fluctuations in autonomous demand. World recessions and booms are frequently, but not always, associated with similar developments in the domestic economy.
2. Monetary policy, in an open economy, can often be seen to operate through the channel of fluctuations in the real exchange rate.

Both these issues will be addressed in this chapter, the plan of which is as follows. In Sec. 8.2 we review some important empirical regularities, or stylized facts, which have stimulated research into open-economy macroeconomics. This is followed, in Sec. 8.3, by an introduction to the Mundell–Fleming model of the open economy, for many years the mainstay of open economic macroeconomic theory. In Sec. 8.4 we present the Dornbusch model of the open economy. This model builds on and extends the Mundell–Fleming model· by allowing for flexible prices and rational expectations in the foreign-exchange market.

8.2 Stylized facts of the open economy

Any theory of the open economy, and of the exchange rate in particular, must take into account two important facts:

1. Although changes in relative prices do seem to affect the exchange rate, the period of time over which this occurs is measured in decades rather than weeks or months.
2. Under a freely floating system there are substantial short-run movements

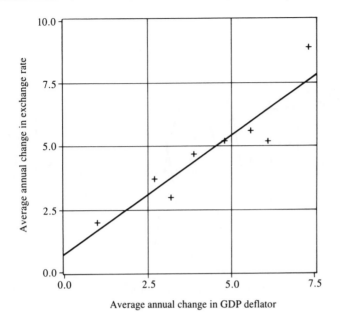

Figure 8.1 Changes in exchange rates and relative prices, 1961–88

in exchange rate which, moreover, appear to be unexpected by participants in the market.

The first hypothesis is equivalent to stating that *purchasing power parity* (PPP) holds in the long run. PPP is the hypothesis that the exchange rate adjusts in order to maintain a constant ratio between national price levels, i.e.:

$$\frac{EP}{P^*} = c \qquad (8.1)$$

where E is the price of a unit of foreign currency, P is the domestic price level, P^* is the foreign price level and c is a constant. We will examine this hypothesis, along with the second in turn, to see if they are supported by empirical evidence.

Figure 8.1 presents some empirical evidence relevant to the first hypothesis. On the horizontal axis we have the average annual change in the GDP deflator for the countries considered relative to that of Germany. These are measured over the period 1960–90. On the vertical axis is the average annual change in the exchange rate of each country relative to the deutschmark. If changes in relative prices are an important determinant of long-run movements in the exchange rate we would expect a close positive

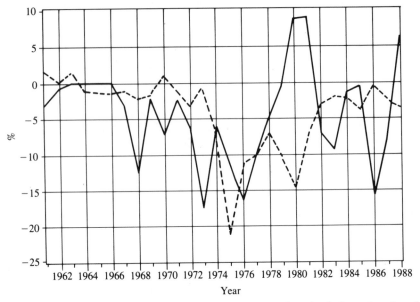

Figure 8.2 Percentage changes in exchange rate (———) and relative prices (– – –)
—UK and Germany, 1961–88. (*Source:* Eurostat)

relationship between the two series. This is, in fact, exactly what we observe.
The scatter points are grouped closely around the best-fit line, indicating a
high degree of association. Estimating the regression equation yields:

$$\Delta E = 0.7179 + 0.9409\Delta P \qquad R^2 = 0.85$$
$$(0.95) \qquad (5.91)$$

t-ratios are in parentheses below the coefficients.

Even given that there are only eight observations, this indicates a very
strong relationship between changes in prices and the nominal exchange
rate relative to Germany. Moreover, the coefficient on the relative price
term is close to unity, indicating a one-for-one trade-off, i.e. a 10 per cent
increase in prices relative to Germany will eventually lead to a 10 per cent
depreciation of the exchange rate.

The evidence above indicates that a long-run relationship between price
movements and exchange rate movements may well exist. However, the
evidence for any short-run link is much weaker. Consider the time series
graph shown in Fig. 8.2. This plots the year-on-year change in the
deutschmark–sterling exchange rate and the year-on-year change in UK
relative to German prices, concentrating on the period of floating exchange
rates from 1972 to 1989. If a short-run relationship were to exist, we would

expect these two series to move closely together. Instead, we observe little or no relationship between them. We must therefore conclude that changes in relative prices do not lead to offsetting changes in the nominal exchange within the same year. Any such effect takes many years to be felt fully.

The chief reason for the failure of relative price movements to play a role in the short-run determination of exchange rates is probably the importance of capital flows between countries. These have increased greatly since the Second World War as capital markets have become more integrated and as exchange controls have been dismantled. Under these circumstances, the exchange rate plays the role of ensuring that the returns on assets in different countries are equalized, rather than the relative price of goods. This role is summarized in the *uncovered interest parity (UIP) condition*. This is written as:

$$r = r^* + \frac{\Delta E^e}{E} \tag{8.2}$$

This equation states that for asset returns to be equalized across countries the domestic rate of interest must equal the foreign rate plus the expected change in the value of the domestic currency relative to the foreign currency. It illustrates immediately why monetary policies, both at home and abroad, are likely to have effects on the exchange rate. Changes in the rate of interest produced by monetary interventions require the exchange rate to move in such a way as to satisfy Eq. (8.2) in a world of freely mobile capital.

Despite the analysis of the previous paragraph, it is arguable that most of the exchange-rate movements which actually take place are not anticipated by market participants. The evidence for this derives from inferences made about expectations by the behaviour of agents in the forward exchange markets. If agents are risk-neutral then the amount they will be willing to pay for delivery of foreign currency at a future date will equal their expectations of the spot exchange rate at that date. This can be written:

$$_t f_{t+1} = {_t}s^e_{t+1} \tag{8.3}$$

where $_t f_{t+1}$ is the forward exchange rate at date t for delivery at date $t + 1$ and $_t s^e_{t+1}$ is the expectation of the spot rate at date $t + 1$, formed at date t (both variables are expressed in natural logarithms). If we assume rational expectations then expectations are formed using all available information, and therefore:

$$_t s^e_{t+1} = s_{t+1} + v_{t+1} \tag{8.4}$$

where v_{t+1} is a stochastic error term which is independent of all information dated t or earlier. Combining Eqs. (8.3) and (8.4) yields a model which can be empirically tested in the form:

$$s_t = b_0 + b_1{}_{t-1}f_t + v_t \tag{8.4a}$$

If the forward rate is to measure expectations about the future spot rate then we should obtain coefficients $b_0 = 0$ and $b_1 = 1$ for this model. Numerous empirical studies have confirmed that this holds in a wide variety of situations.

8.3 A short-run model with sticky prices

We have seen in the empirical section that any theoretical model of the open economy must embody the following features:

1. The existence of a long-run relationship between relative prices in different countries and the exchange rate between them, but the possibility of substantial short-run deviations from this relationship.
2. Volatile short-run movements in the exchange rate which are not predicted by market participants, i.e. responses to 'news'.
3. Interactions between the monetary policies pursued by national governments, the nominal and real exchange rates and the level of real activity.

The model presented below is that developed separately by Mundell and Fleming during the early 1960s. Although it now has a long history, the model is still influential in guiding the thinking of macroeconomists and provides a powerful and flexible tool for policy analysis. The first equation (8.5) describes the demand for goods. This is assumed to depend on the real exchange rate, or the level of competitiveness, and the rate of interest. For simplicity, it is assumed that the steady-state rate of inflation is zero. This enables us to neglect the difference between the nominal and real rates of interest. We also include a shift parameter, α, in the equation which allows for exogenous shifts in aggregate demand. These could be due to factors such as changes in fiscal policy or shifts in export demand which are unrelated to changes in the real exchange rate:

$$y = \alpha + \beta(e + p^* - p) - \gamma r \tag{8.5}$$

The second equation is a conventional demand for money function relating the demand for real money balances to the level of aggregate demand and the rate of interest:

$$m - p = ky - \lambda r \tag{8.6}$$

These first two equations represent a simple extension of the *IS–LM* model to the open economy. Equation (8.5) is an *IS* curve in which we have allowed for the effects of the real exchange rate on aggregate demand while

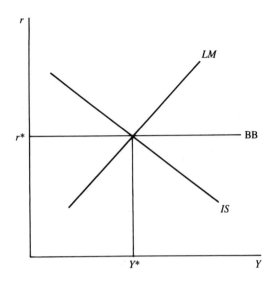

Figure 8.3 The Mundell–Fleming model

Eq. (8.6) is a perfectly standard *LM* curve. To solve the model for the open-economy case, however, we also need to make some assumption about the link between the rate of interest and the capital account of the balance of payments. The simplest assumption to make is that there is perfect capital mobility, so that the uncovered interest parity condition must hold. This effectively means that when we draw the standard *IS–LM* diagram as in Fig. 8.3 we must add a third equilibrium condition in the form of the horizontal line going through the world interest rate. If the interest rate differs from the world rate, and this is not compensated for by an expected change in the value of the exchange rate, then the balance of payments will either be in surplus or deficit due to the existence of a capital inflow or outflow.

   In the early 1960s Mundell and Fleming analysed the type of economy described in the previous paragraph. They made the simplifying assumption of static expectations, i.e. that the expected change in the exchange rate is always zero. This is somewhat unsatisfactory, since it is clearly inconsistent with the principle of rational expectations. However, for the moment, we will maintain this assumption and relax it in the next section, when we go on to look at Dornbusch's (1976) extension of the Mundell–Fleming model.

   The reaction of the Mundell–Fleming economy to disturbances depends on the exchange rate regime in place. We will consider two kinds of shock to the economy. The first is a world recession which reduces the demand for domestic exports and the second is an increase in the foreign rate of interest.

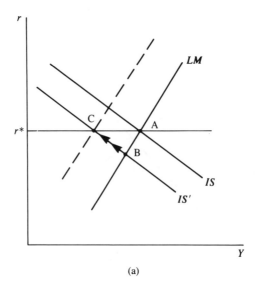

(a)

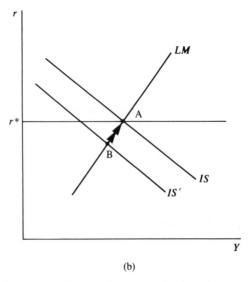

(b)

Figure 8.4 Reaction to world recession. (a) Fixed exchange rate; (b) flexible exchange rate

A reduction in the demand for exports will cause the *IS* curve to shift backwards, as in Fig. 8.4. Consider first Fig. 8.4(a): the new impact equilibrium is at point B, where the new *IS* curve (*IS'*) crosses the original

LM curve. At point B the interest rate is lower than the foreign rate, which means that reserves are being lost because of the outflow of capital. There is therefore a further dynamic effect on the equilibrium, coming through the shrinking of the domestic money stock, caused by the reduction in the monetary base due to the loss of foreign exchange reserves. In diagrammatic terms, the *LM* curve shifts backwards and continues to do so until the loss of reserves ceases. This occurs when the rate of interest has risen once more to the level of the foreign rate.

The reaction of the economy to a world recession is quite different under a flexible exchange-rate regime. Although the impact equilibrium is the same, as shown in Fig. 8.4(b), the subsequent dynamic effects work in the opposite direction. At point B but with flexible exchange rates the loss of foreign exchange reserves puts pressure on the exchange rate to depreciate rather than causing the money stock to fall. With fixed prices the depreciation leads to gains in competitiveness, which cause the *IS* curve to shift backwards towards its original position. It is straightforward to see that the *IS* curve will continue shifting until the rate of interest is once more at the world level and output has risen back to its original level. Thus one of the benefits claimed for a flexible exchange-rate regime is that it is better at insulating the economy from foreign shocks to aggregate demand, in comparison with a fixed exchange-rate regime, which tends to amplify such shocks.

The differences between exchange-rate regimes are even more noticeable when we consider the reaction of the economy to an increase in the foreign rate of interest. Consider Fig. 8.5. Figure 8.5(a) shows the reaction of the economy under fixed exchange rates. The rise in foreign rates produces a capital outflow, a reduction of the money stock and a fall in output, in much the same way as the reduction in exports did in the previous case. The path of the economy through time is indicated by the arrows in the figure. Now consider the same change in the foreign interest rate but with a flexible exchange rate, as shown in Fig. 8.5(b). Here the loss of reserves leads to a depreciation of the exchange rate which in turn causes the economy to expand because of the gain in competitiveness.

Two other experiments can be easily carried out using this framework. If the government increases the money stock then it can be shown that output will increase if the exchange rate is flexible, but remain constant if it is fixed. Similarly, it can be shown that, if government expenditure is increased, output will increase if the exchange rate is fixed, but remain constant if it is flexible. The mechanics of working through the figure for these two cases are left as exercises for the interested reader.

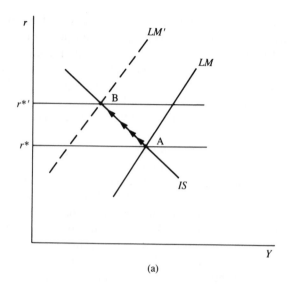

(a)

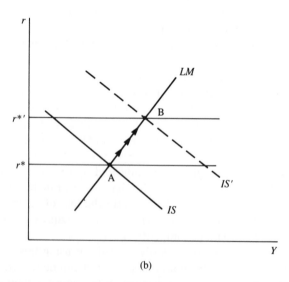

(b)

Figure 8.5 Reaction to increase in foreign interest rate. (a) Fixed exchange rate; (b) flexible exchange rate

8.4 A long-run model with flexible prices

In the previous section we assumed a fixed price level to solve for the effects of changes in the exogenous variables of the model on output and interest rates.[1] We will now consider the same model but with flexible prices and with rational expectations about exchange-rate movements.

To do this, we make use of the following pair of dynamic equations in exchange rates and prices:

$$de/dt = r - r^* \qquad (8.7)$$

This equation is the uncovered interest parity condition expressed in continuous rather than discrete time. The economy is assumed to be small relative to the rest of the world, which implies that the foreign rate of interest is exogenous to any events taking place within the domestic economy. Finally, the model is completed by specifying a dynamic equation for the evolution of prices, as shown by

$$dp/dt = \delta(y - y_n) \qquad (8.8)$$

This equation can be thought of as a type of Phillips curve. The rate of change of prices is determined by the state of excess demand. If demand is too large for the natural level of output then prices rise, while if it falls short then prices fall. Since we assume that the steady-state rate of inflation is zero then we do not need to include any term in expected inflation. Buiter and Miller (1981) have relaxed this assumption by allowing for steady-state inflation in the Dornbusch model, and have shown that it does not alter the general properties of the model in any significant way.

Although these dynamic equations look superficially similar, they are in fact fundamentally different in character. The exchange rate constitutes a *jump variable*, by which we mean that the value taken by the exchange rate at any particular point in time is not tied down by its previous history. If new information becomes available which is relevant to the determination of the exchange rate, it can jump immediately in response to this. In contrast, the price level is assumed to respond sluggishly to changes in its determinants. A possible reason for this is the existence of staggered contracts of the type discussed in Chapter 5. It is this combination of a perfectly flexible exchange rate with a slowly adjusting price level which produces the overshooting result characteristic of the Dornbusch model.

Now that we have the building blocks in place, we can put the model together to analyse its dynamic properties. In order to make use of a graphical approach we will make the simplifying assumption that output is always at the natural, or full, employment level. Once again, this assumption is made for reasons of tractability only. In fact, Dornsbusch (1976) shows in the appendix to his paper that relaxing this assumption does not change the

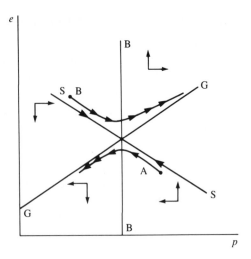

Figure 8.6 Phase diagram for the Dornbusch model

qualitative results of the model at all, but it does simplify the algebra to a considerable extent and permits a simple graphical exposition of the model. The diagram we will use shows the determination of the exchange rate and the price level, along with their evolution through time in response to a variety of disturbances. It is an example of a type of graphical device known as a *phase diagram*, designed to show the motion through time of the endogenous variables of a simultaneous equations system. Figure 8.6 shows the phase diagram for this model. On the axes we have the exchange rate and the price level.

To determine the equilibrium of the system we first solve for the combinations of the exchange rate and the price level which are consistent with stable prices. This is done by using the demand for money function (8.6) to eliminate the rate of interest from the aggregate demand equation (8.5) and then setting aggregate demand equal to the natural level of output y_n. From this we obtain an upward-sloping relationship between the exchange rate and the price level as shown by the GG line in Fig. 8.6. The second step of our analysis is to find the set of values of the exchange rate and the price level which are consistent with a stable exchange rate. This in fact is somewhat easier than the previous case. For stable exchange rates we require the uncovered interest parity condition to be satisfied while the exchange rate remains constant. This in turn requires that the domestic rate of interest equal the foreign rate, and from the demand for money function we see that there is a unique price level at which this latter condition is satisfied. Therefore the vertical line marked BB in Fig. 8.6 is the second of our equilibrium conditions. The intersection of the stable price line with the stable exchange rate line determines the equilibrium of the system. We can use this diagram to conduct conventional comparative static experiments (for example, to fing the long-run effects of increasing the money stock and government expenditure). It can also be used to examine the effects of changing the other exogenous variables, such as the foreign rate of interest or the foreign price level. However, our main focus of interest will be on the dynamic path towards the long-run equilibrium.

The diagram shows the way in which the two variables move when the economy is not in full equilibrium by the use of arrows of motion. To the right of the BB locus the interest rate is higher than the foreign rate, since the level of real-money balances is low because of the high price level. This means that the exchange rate must be rising (depreciating) in order to maintain the uncovered interest parity condition, and thus the arrows of motion show an upward movement in *e*. Now consider the GG locus. Above this curve the value of the exchange rate is too low for the level of aggregate demand to be equal to the natural level of output, and there is therefore a state of excess demand and prices are rising. Below the curve the exchange rate is overvalued, demand is too low and prices are therefore falling. Using this information, we can draw arrows of motion for all the possible regions of the phase diagram.

The question we now wish to address is whether the economy will converge on the long-run equilibrium from any particular point in the phase plane. We can see clearly that in two of the four regions of the diagram, that to the right of BB and above GG and that to the left of BB and below GG, convergence is impossible, since both the arrows of motion point away from the equilibrium point. In the other two regions the arrows of motion are such that convergence is possible but by no means certain. Consider path A in the diagram. If we start the economy at some arbitrary point, then it may appear to move towards the equilibrium for some time but eventually it crosses into the region to the left of BB and below GG. Here motion is uniformly away from the stable point. Similarly, along path B, the economy approaches the equilibrium for some time but eventually passes into the region to the right of BB and above GG, at which stage it moves continuously away from the equilibrium. In fact, it can be shown that there exists a unique convergent path to the equilibrium, as shown by the line marked SS in the diagram. If the economy does not begin on the SS path then it must eventually become unstable, moving cumulatively away from equilibrium. The SS path is frequently referred to by its technical name of the *stable manifold.*

Let us begin by considering the effects of a domestic monetary expansion, illustrated in Fig. 8.7. From our pair of long-run equilibrium conditions we

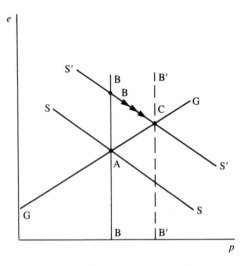

Figure 8.7 Monetary expansion in the Dornbusch model

see that this shifts the BB locus to the right, since an increase in price is needed to restore the level of real-money balances to its initial value and hence to keep the domestic interest rate equal to the foreign rate. The new equilibrium is therefore one in which prices have risen and the exchange rate has depreciated by the same proportion. Passing through the new equilibrium point is a new stable manifold marked S'S'.

The dynamic path to the new equilibrium can be traced as follows. Following the monetary expansion, the price level is initially fixed. However, the economy must move immediately onto the new stable manifold if it is to converge on the new equilibrium. The only way in which this can be achieved is for the exchange rate to jump immediately to a new higher value, as at point B on the diagram. After the impact effect of the monetary expansion there is a period during which the economy experiences excess demand and rising prices. During this period the economy moves down the new stable manifold from point B towards the new equilibrium point C.

It is worth examining the characteristics of the transition path of the economy a little more closely. One of the apparent paradoxes of a monetary expansion is that it requires a depreciation of the exchange rate to take place to offset the effects of higher prices of competitiveness. However, at the same time, an increase in the money stock lowers interest rates which in turn means that the exchange rate must be appreciating through time if the uncovered interest parity condition is to remain satisfied. The transition path in the diagram reconciles these two apparently conflicting requirements.

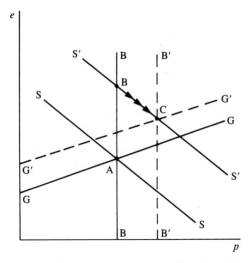

Figure 8.8 Increase in the foreign interest in the Dornbusch model

In moving from the initial equilibrium point A to the impact equilibrium point B the exchange rate overshoots its long-run equilibrium value. During the transition period the interest rate is lower than the foreign rate because real-money balances are high. Despite this, however, the uncovered interest parity condition is satisfied because the exchange rate is depreciating along the stable manifold.

As an alternative case, let us consider the effects of an increase in the foreign interest rate. This shifts both the GG and BB loci. The GG locus shifts upwards because the increase in the foreign interest rate reduces demand and hence a higher degree of competitiveness becomes necessary to maintain the equality between aggregate demand and the natural level of output. The BB locus shifts to the right because the domestic rate of interest must rise to match the increase in the foreign rate. This in turn requires the price level to rise to reduce the stock of real-money balances in line with the reduction in demand. The combination of these two shifts produces a new long-run equilibrium in which the domestic price level rises and the exchange rate depreciates.

The path to the new equilibrium is illustrated in Fig. 8.8. Initial equilibrium is at point A. When the foreign interest rate rises there is a new long-run equilibrium at point C and a new stable manifold going through this point. Since prices are sticky the exchange rate initially jumps to point B. At point B there is excess demand and prices begin to rise. This drives the economy along the new stable manifold until it reaches long-run equilibrium at point C.

Unit 8.1

How predictable is the exchange rate?

In common with many financial assets, there exists a forward market in foreign currency. This means that agents within the market can arrange to buy and sell foreign currency for delivery at some future date. One advantage of this for the economist investigating these markets is that we can use observations on the prices being charged in forward markets to make inferences about what agents expect to happen in future spot markets.

Consider the choice facing an agent who wishes to obtain a given supply of deutschmarks in a month's time. He or she can purchase them now in the forward market or wait and purchase them in the spot market when the time comes around. If they are cheaper in the forward market than they are expected to be in the future spot market then this method will be preferred and vice versa. Agents will only be indifferent between the two methods when the current forward price equals the expected future spot price. If there is a competitive market then arbitrage will ensure that this equality is brought about.

We can use the relationship between the spot and the forward rates to conduct a series of interesting tests of economic theory. First, we can test if the lagged forward rate is a good predictor of the future spot rate in the way that the theory suggests. Figure U8.1.1 shows the spot sterling–deutschmark exchange rate and the lagged forward rate using monthly data over the period February

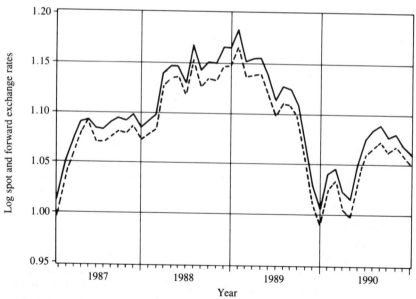

Figure U8.1.1 Log of spot pound (———)–deutschmark exchange rate and log of forward rate (– – –). (*Source:* Datastream)

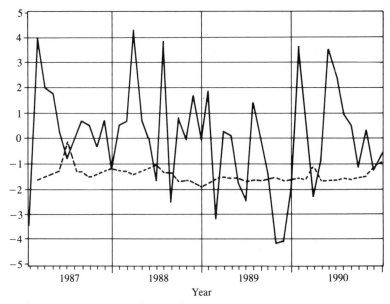

Figure U8.1.2 Change in spot pound (————)–deutschmark exchange rate and lagged forward premium (– – –). (*Source:* Datastream)

1987 to January 1991. Examination of this figure clearly indicates some sort of relationship between the two series. However, we can obtain a more precise idea of the strength of the relationship by regressing one variable against the other, as shown below:

$$LS_t = 0.1284 + 0.8952 LF_{t-1}$$
$$\quad\;\; (0.07) \quad (0.06) \qquad\qquad\qquad\qquad \text{(U8.1.1)}$$

$$R^2 = 0.81 \qquad DW = 1.72$$

Standard errors are given in parentheses below the coefficients.

The equation produces results which closely conform to economic theory. The coefficient on the lagged forward rate is insignificantly different from one at the 5 per cent level, while the constant is insignificantly different from zero at the same level (though it is on the borderline of significance). In addition, the equation fits well, as shown by the high R^2, and there is no evidence of residual autocorrelation.

Evidence suggests, therefore, that the forward rate is an unbiased predictor of the future spot rate. However, this does not necessarily mean that it is a good predictor. To see why this is the case, let us turn to Fig. U8.1.2, which shows the month-on-month changes in the exchange rate and the lagged forward premium during this period. The forward premium is the percentage difference between the forward and spot rates. We see from this figure that most of the actual changes in the exchange rate which took place were not incorporated into the forward exchange rate. In other words, they seem to have taken market participants by surprise. We must therefore conclude that most exchange-rate movements on a month-to-month basis are not predictable. This does not necessarily mean that longer-run movements are unpredictable since we have seen that countries with persistently high inflation rates tend to have depreciating currencies.

Unit 8.2

Rational expectations and speculative bubbles

When the international monetary system moved to one of floating exchange rates in the early 1970s it quickly became obvious that the possibility of making short-term capital gains by trading in the foreign exchange market was just as important in the determination of the exchange rate as so-called 'market fundamentals' such as relative prices. Speculative bubbles became an all-too-real fact of life facing national governments trying to manage their economies.

How can we model speculative bubbles in the exchange rate? One method is to include the expected gain from holding foreign currency in its demand function. So, for example, suppose the demand for foreign currency takes the form:

$$d_t = a - be_t + c\Delta e^e_{t-1} \tag{U8.2.1}$$

where e_t is the exchange rate at date t and Δe^e_{t+1} is the expected change in the exchange rate. Suppose, for simplicity, there is a fixed supply of foreign exchange available equal to s. The market fundamentals solution is obtained by solving for the equality of demand with supply when the expected change in the exchange rate is zero. This yields:

$$\bar{e} = (a - s)/b \tag{U8.2.2}$$

However, it is possible to think of solutions in which a speculative demand for currency keeps the exchange rate away from its market fundamental value. This will occur when the expected change in e is non-zero. When this is the case we can solve for the expected time path of exchange rates to obtain:

$$e^e_{t+1} = [(b + c)/c]e_t - (a - s)/c \tag{U8.2.3}$$

This type of equation appears to capture the main features of a speculative bubble in that it generates an explosive movement away from the market fundamental solution, which is determined simply by the expectation of a continuing rise in the value of foreign currency. It is essentially the same model as that of Flood and Garber (1980).

The problem with Eq. (U8.2.3) is that it cannot be consistent with rational expectations unless the bubble is expected to continue for ever. If market participants acknowledge even the possibility of a crash of the bubble to the fundamentals solution then the time path implied by the equation cannot be a rational expectation. However, Blanchard (1979) has provided an alternative formulation in which agents recognize the probability of a crash in the market and allow for this. The main modification is that the demand curve for foreign currency will now take the form:

$$d_t = a - be_t + c\pi\Delta e_{t+1}^e \qquad (U8.2.4)$$

where π is the probability that the bubble will continue. The solution for the time path of the exchange rate also has a similar solution except that πc now appears on the denominator of the lagged exchange-rate term. The advantage of this formulation is that it is now consistent with rational expectations, since agents now recognize that the bubble will burst within some finite time period. However, they also believe that there is some probability that it will continue into the next time period, and that there are therefore possible gains to be made by holding on to foreign currency even when it is overvalued relative to market fundamentals.

Review questions

1. Consider the following simple fixed-price model of the economy:

$$y = 0.75(e + p^* - p) - 0.25r \qquad \textit{IS curve}$$

$$m - p = y - 0.5r \qquad \textit{LM curve}$$

$$r = r^* = 0.05 \qquad \text{Interest parity condition}$$

These equations describe an economy in which the exchange rate is expected to remain fixed. All variables are in natural logarithms except for the interest rate.

(a) If $m = p = p^* = 0$, compute the level of output which yields money market equilibrium and hence the exchange rate which will simultaneously yield goods market equilibrium.

(b) Suppose that, due to a change of government, the market expects the exchange rate to be devalued by 5 per cent in the next period. What are the immediate effects on the level of output and the exchange rate?

2. Consider the following simple flexible price model of the economy:

$$y_n = 0.75(e + p^* - p) - 0.25r$$

$$m - p = y_n - 0.5r$$

Output is fixed exogenously at the natural level 0, $p^* = m = 0$ and the foreign rate of interest is 3 per cent.

(a) What will be the long-run equilibrium levels of prices and the exchange rate?

   (b) Describe, using diagrams, the adjustment of the economy to an increase in the money stock when price adjustment is determined according to a conventional Phillips curve equation.

3. Discuss the relationship of the Dornbusch open-economy model to the earlier Mundell–Fleming model.

4. Trace the way in which a foreign monetary expansion would affect domestic output in the Mundell–Fleming model with fixed exchange rates and in the same model with flexible exchange rates.

5. For a highly open economy like that of Britain fluctuations in exports are an important source of business-cycle fluctuations. The table below gives percentage changes in GDP and exports for the UK. Try plotting the two series on a graph to see how close is the relationship between them.

UK: percentage changes GDP and exports

	GDP	Exports
1961	3.3	3.1
1962	1.0	1.8
1963	4.2	4.3
1964	5.1	3.2
1965	2.3	4.5
1966	1.9	4.0
1967	2.8	1.5
1968	4.1	12.0
1969	0.8	8.9
1970	2.9	4.9
1971	2.7	7.0
1972	2.3	0.4
1973	7.7	11.6
1974	−1.0	6.8
1975	−0.6	−2.8
1976	3.8	8.7
1977	1.1	6.2
1978	3.6	1.7
1979	2.1	4.0
1980	−2.1	−0.3
1981	−1.2	−0.8
1982	1.1	0.7
1983	3.5	2.1
1984	2.0	6.9
1985	3.7	5.5
1986	2.9	3.2
1987	3.6	6.2
1988	4.4	0.7

Source: Eurostat

Note

1. *Equilibrium solution of the Dornbusch model*
   In the steady-state equilibrium output must equal the natural level and the rate of interest must equal the foreign rate. We can therefore solve for the effects of changes in exogenous variables on the equilibrium values of the exchange rate and the price level. Our pair of equilibrium relationships can be written as follows:

$$y_n = \alpha + \beta(e + p^* - p) - \gamma r^*$$

$$m - p = ky_n - \lambda r^*$$

e and p are endogenous while y_n, p^*, r^* and m are exogenous. Solving for e and p, we have:

$$p = m - ky_n + \lambda r^*$$

$$e = (m - ky_n + \lambda r^*) - p^* + (y_n + \gamma r^*)/\beta$$

The second of these equations can be simplified by noting that the first expression in parentheses is equal to the equilibrium solution for the price level given by the first equation. Hence we can write:

$$e = (p - p^*) + (y_n + \gamma r^*)/\beta$$

The first part of this expression is the purchasing power parity formula. However, the presence of the other terms indicates that this relationship can be disturbed by changes in the natural level of output or the foreign interest rate. The equilibrium solutions can be used to work out the long-run effects of changes in the exogenous variables on the exchange rate and the price level. These are given in the table below.

Long-run elasticities in the Dornbusch model

	e	p
y_n	$-(\beta k - 1)/\beta$	$-k$
α	$-1/\beta$	0
m	1	1
p^*	-1	0
r^*	$(\beta\lambda + \gamma)/\beta$	λ

Bibliography

Adelman, Irma, 'Business cycles—endogenous or stochastic?' *Economic Journal*, Vol. 70, 1960, pp. 783–96.

Adelman, Irma and Frank L. Adelman, 'The dynamic properties of the Klein–Goldberger model', *Econometrica*, Vol. 27, No. 4, October 1959, pp. 596–625.

Akerlof, George and Janet Yellen, 'A near rational model of the business cycle with wage and price inertia', *Quarterly Journal of Economics*, Vol. 101, 1985, pp. 823–38.

Alogoskoufis, George and Ron Smith, 'The Phillips curve, the persistence of inflation and the Lucas critique: evidence from exchange rate regimes', *American Economic Review*, Vol. 81, December 1991, pp. 1254–75.

Artis, M. J. and M. K. Lewis, 'How unstable is the demand for money in the United Kingdom?' *Economica*, Vol. 51, 1984, pp. 473–6.

Barro, Robert, 'Are government bonds net wealth?' *Journal of Political Economy*, Vol. 82, 1974, pp. 1095–1117.

Barro, Robert, 'Unanticipated money, output, and the price level in the United States', *Journal of Political Economy*, Vol. 86, 1978, pp. 549–80.

Baumol, William J., 'The transactions demand for cash: an inventory theoretic approach', *Quarterly Journal of Economics*, Vol. 66, 1952, pp. 545–56.

Baumol, William J. and Jess Benhabib, 'Chaos: significance, mechanism and econometric applications', *Journal of Economic Perspectives*, Vol. 3, No. 1, Winter 1989, pp. 77–105.

Blackburn, Keith and Morten Ravn, 'Business cycles in the UK: facts and fictions', mimeo, University of Southampton, November 1990.

Blanchard, Olivier, 'Speculative bubbles, crashes and rational expectations', *Economics Letters*, Vol. 3, 1979, pp. 387–89.

Blanchard, Olivier and Lawrence Summers, 'Hysteresis and the European unemployment problem', *NBER Macroeconomics Annual*, 1986, pp. 15–77.

Blaug, Mark, *Economic Theory in Retrospect*, Cambridge University Press, 4th ed., 1985.

Buiter, Willem and Marcus Miller, 'Monetary policy and international competitiveness', *Oxford Economic Papers*, Vol. 33 (Supplement), 1981, pp. 143–75.

Campbell, J. Y. and N. G. Mankiw, 'Are output fluctuations transitory?' *Quarterly Journal of Economics*, Vol. 102, 1987, pp. 857–80.

Davidson, James, David Hendry, Frank Srba and Stephen Yeo, 'Econometric modelling of the aggregate time-series relationship between consumers' expenditure and income in the United Kingdom', *Economic Journal*, Vol. 88, December 1978, pp. 661–92.

De Long, J. Bradford and Lawrence Summers, 'Is increased price flexibility stabilizing?' *American Economic Review*, Vol. 76, 1986, pp. 1031–44.

Dickey, D. A. and W. A. Fuller, 'Distribution of the estimators for autoregressive time series with a unit root', *Journal of the American Statistical Association*, Vol. 74, 1979, pp. 427–31.

Dornbusch, Rudiger, 'Expectations and exchange rate dynamics', *Journal of Political Economy*, Vol. 84, 1976, pp. 1161–76.

Fisher, Irving, *The Purchasing Power of Money*, Macmillan, 1927.

Fleming, J. M., 'Domestic financial policies under fixed and flexible exchange rates', *International Monetary Fund Staff Papers*, Vol. 9, 1962, pp. 369–79.

Flood, R. and P. Garber, 'Market fundamentals versus price level bubbles: the first tests', *Journal of Political Economy*, 1980.

Friedman, Milton, 'The role of monetary policy', *American Economic Review*, Vol. 38, 1968, pp. 1–17.

Friedman, Milton, *A Theoretical Framework for Monetary Analysis*, National Bureau for Economic Research, New York, 1971.

Frisch, Ragnar, 'Propagation and impulse problems in dynamic economics', in *Economic Essays in Honour of Gustav Cassel*, Allen and Unwin, 1937.

Harvey, Andrew C., 'Trends and cycles in macroeconomic time series', *Journal of Business Economics and Statistics*, Vol. 3, No. 3, July 1985, pp. 216–27.

Hendry, David and Grayham Mizon, 'Serial correlation as a convenient simplification, not a nuisance: a comment on a study of the demand for money by the Bank of England', *Economic Journal*, Vol. 88, September 1978, pp. 549–63.

Hicks, John, R., 'Mr Keynes and the "Classics": a suggested interpretation', *Econometrica*, Vol. 5, April 1937, pp. 147–59.

Keynes, John Maynard, *The General Theory of Employment, Interest and Money*, Macmillan, 1936.

Klein, L. R. and A. S. Goldberger, *An Econometric Model of the United States 1929–1952*, North-Holland, 1955.

Kydland, F. E. and E. C. Prescott, 'Business cycles: real facts and a monetary myth', *Federal Reserve Bank of Minneapolis Quarterly Review*, Spring 1990, pp. 3–18.

Layard, R. and S. Nickell, 'Unemployment in Britain', *Economica* Supplement, 53, 1986, pp. 121–169.

Lucas, R. E., Jr, 'Expectations and the neutrality of money', *Journal of Economic Theory*, Vol. 90, 1972, pp., 103–24.

Lucas, Robert, E., Jr, 'Some international evidence of output–inflation tradeoffs', *American Economic Review*, Vol. 63, June 1973, pp. 326–34.

Lucas, R. E., Jr, 'Econometric policy evaluations: a critique', in Brunner, K. and A. Meltzer (eds), *The Phillips Curve and the Labour Market*, North Holland, 1976.

Lucas, Robert E., Jr, 'Understanding business cycles', in *Stabilization of the Domestic and International Economy, Carnegie–Rochester Series on Public Policy*, Vol. 5, 1977, pp. 7–30.

Lucas, Robert E., Jr and Leonard A. Rapping, 'Real wages, employment and growth', *Journal of Political Economy*, Vol. 77, No. 5, 1969.

McDonald, Garry and David Turner, 'The PC-ready reckoner program manual', ESRC Macroeconomic Modelling Bureau (mimeo), March 1990.

Malthus, T., *An Essay on the Principle of Population*, 1798, reprinted London: MacMillan, 1926.

Mankiw, N. Gregory, 'Small menu costs and large business cycles: a macroeconomic model of monopoly', *Quarterly Journal of Economics*, Vol. 100, 1985, pp. 225–52.

Mankiw, N. Gregory, 'Real business cycles: a new Keynesian perspective', *Journal of Economic Perspectives*, Vol. 3, No. 3, Summer 1989, pp. 79–90.

Manning, A., 'Implicit contract theory', Chapter 4 of Sapsford, D. and Z. Tzannatos (eds), *Current Issues in Labour Economics*, MacMillan, 1990.

May, R. M., 'Simple mathematical model with very complicated dynamics', *Nature*, Vol. 261, 1976, pp. 459–67.

Mills, Terence C., *Time Series Techniques for Economists*, Cambridge University Press, 1990.

Modigliani, Franco, 'Liquidity preference and the theory of interest and money', *Econometrica*, 1944.

Morgan, Mary S., *The History of Econometric Ideas*, Cambridge University Press, 1990.

Mundell, Robert, 'Capital mobility and stabilization policy under fixed and flexible exchange rates', *Canadian Journal of Economics and Political Science*, Vol. 29, 1963, pp. 475–85.

Nelson, Charles R. and Heejoon Kang, 'Spurious periodicity in inappropriately detrended time series', *Econometrica*, Vol. 49, 1981, pp. 741–51.

Nelson, Charles R. and C. I. Plosser, 'Trends and random walks in macroeconomic time series', *Journal of Monetary Economics*, 1982, pp. 129–62.

Oulton, Nicholas, 'Aggregate investment and Tobin's *Q*: the evidence from Britain', *Oxford Economic Papers*, Vol. 33, 1981, pp. 177–202.

Perron, Pierre, 'The Great Crash, the oil price shock and the unit root hypothesis, *Econometrica*, Vol. 57, No. 6, November 1989, pp. 1361–1401.

Phillips, A. W., 'The relation between unemployment and the rate of change of money wage rates in the United Kingdom, 1861–1957', *Economica*, Vol. 25, 1958, pp. 283–300.

Plosser, Charles, I., 'Understanding real business cycles', *Journal of Economic Perspectives*, Vol. 3, No. 3, Summer 1989, pp. 51–77.

Prescott, Edward, 'Theory ahead of business cycle measurement', *Carnegie-Rochester Series on Public Policy*, Vol. 25, Autumn 1986, pp. 11–44.

Rappoport, P. and L. Reichlin, 'Segmented trends and non-stationary time series', *Economic Journal Conference Supplement*, Vol. 90, 1989, pp. 168–77.

Romer, Paul, 'Increasing returns and long-run growth', *Journal of Political Economy*, Vol. 94, 1986, pp. 1002–37.

Romer, Paul, 'Crazy explanations for the productivity slowdown', *NBER Macroeconomics Annual*, 1986a.

Samuelson, Paul A., 'Interactions between the multiplier process and the principle of acceleration', *Review of Economic Statistics*, Vol. 21, May 1939, pp. 75–8.

Sargent, Thomas and Neil Wallace, 'Rational expectations and the theory of economic policy', *Journal of Monetary Economics*, Vol. 2, 1976, pp. 169–83.

Shapiro, Carl and Joseph Stiglitz, 'Equilibrium unemployment as a worker-discipline device', *American Economic Review*, Vol. 74, 1984, pp. 433–44.

Slutsky, E. E., 'The summation of random causes as the source of business cycles', *Econometrica*, Vol. 5, 1937, pp. 105–46.

Solow, Robert, 'Technical change and the aggregate production function', *Review of Economics and Statistics,* Vol. 39, 1957, pp. 312–20.

Taylor, John, 'Staggered wage setting in a macroeconomic model', *American Economic Review*, Vol. 69, 1979, pp. 108-13.

Taylor, John, 'Aggregate demand and staggered contracts', *Journal of Political Economy*, Vol. 88, 1980, pp. 1–23.

Temin, P., *Did Monetary Forces Cause the Great Depression?*, New York: Norton, 1976.

Tobin, James, 'The interest-elasticity of transactions demand for cash', *Review of Economics and Statistics*, Vol. 38, 1956, pp. 241–47.

Tobin, James, 'A general equilibrium approach to monetary theory', *Journal of Money Credit and Banking*, Vol. 1, 1969, pp. 15–29.

Tobin, James, 'Keynesian models of recession and depression', *American Economic Review: Papers and Proceedings*, Vol. 65, 1975, pp. 195–202.

Tobin, James, *Asset Accumulation and Economic Activity*, Basil Blackwell, 1980.

Wallis, Kenneth F. (ed.), *Models of the UK Economy: A Review by the ESRC Macroeconomic Modelling Bureau*, Oxford University Press, 1989.

Index